Professional Development for Language Teachers

CAMBRIDGE LANGUAGE EDUCATION
Series Editor: Jack C. Richards

Professional Development for Language Teachers

Strategies for Teacher Learning

Jack C. Richards
SEAMEO Regional Language Centre

Thomas S. C. Farrell
Brock University

CAMBRIDGE
UNIVERSITY PRESS

CAMBRIDGE UNIVERSITY PRESS
Cambridge, New York, Melbourne, Madrid, Cape Town, Singapore, São Paulo

Cambridge University Press
40 West 20th Street, New York, NY 10011-4211, USA

www.cambridge.org
Information on this title: www.cambridge.org/9780521849111

First published 2005

Printed in the United States of America

A catalog record for this book is available from the British Library.

Library of Congress Cataloging in Publication Data

Richards, Jack C.
   Professional development for language teachers : strategies for teacher learning / Jack C.
   Richards, Thomas S. C. Farrell.
      p.   cm. – (Cambridge language education)
   Includes bibliographical references and index.
   ISBN-13: 978-0-521-84911-1 (alk. paper)
   ISBN-10: 0-521-84911-X (alk. paper)
   ISBN-13: 978-0-521-61383-5 (pb.)
   ISBN-10: 0-521-61383-3 (pb.)
      1. Language teachers – Training of.   I. Farrell, Thomas S. C. (Thomas Sylvester Charles)
   II. Title.   III. Series.

   P53.85.R534   2005
   407'.1'1 – dc22   2005041972

ISBN 13 978 0 521 84911 1 hardback
ISBN 10 0 521 84911 X hardback

ISBN 13 978 0 521 61383 5 paperback
ISBN 10 0 521 61383 3 paperback

Contents

Series editor's preface

Second and foreign language teaching provides a career for hundreds of thousands of teachers worldwide, and the vast educational enterprise of English language teaching could not operate effectively without the dedication and effort of such teachers day by day and year by year throughout their careers. Maintaining the interest, creativity, and enthusiasm of experienced language teachers in their profession is one of the challenges faced by program coordinators, school principals, and teacher-educators. Teachers need to expand their roles and responsibilities over time if they are to continue to find language teaching rewarding, and it is the responsibility of schools and other educational institutions to provide opportunities for teachers to develop longer-term career goals and opportunities over time.

The field of language teaching is subject to rapid changes, both as the profession responds to new educational paradigms and trends and as institutions face new challenges as a result of changes in curriculum, national tests, and student needs. As a result, teachers need regular opportunities to update their professional knowledge and skills, that is, their opportunities for professional development. Teachers need to be able to take part in activities such as:

- engaging in self-reflection and evaluation
- developing specialized knowledge and skills about many aspects of teaching
- expanding their knowledge base about research, theory, and issues in teaching
- taking on new roles and responsibilities, such as supervisor or mentor teacher, teacher-researcher, or materials writer
- developing collaborative relationships with other teachers

This book provides a survey of current approaches to professional development for language teachers, particularly for those new to teaching or those who seek opportunities for in-service teacher education. A wide variety of approaches are presented and ways of implementing them illustrated, drawing on the authors' experiences of developing and conducting in-service teacher programs in many parts of the world. Throughout the book, personal accounts by the authors and by teachers who have experience using activities such as journal writing, peer observation, and teaching portfolios provide compelling examples of how and when such activities can be useful and their advantages and limitations.

This book will therefore serve as a useful source book for teachers, teacher-educators, supervisors, teaching mentors, and others who are interested in carrying out teacher-development activities in their own settings.

Jack C. Richards

Preface

This book examines a variety of approaches to professional development for language teachers. In most schools and institutions today, language teachers are expected to keep up to date with developments in the field, to regularly review and evaluate their teaching skills, and to take on new teaching assignments according to the changing needs of the institution. Some teachers may also be expected to serve as mentors to new teachers, to plan workshops and other professional activities, to present papers at seminars or conferences, and to write for journals and teaching magazines. Language teaching institutions are also expected to maintain high professional standards, to provide opportunities for their teachers to pursue professional development, and to provide conditions where teachers cooperate to achieve higher levels of learning among their students.

This book is intended as a practical introduction and guide for teachers, administrators, and coordinators who wish to implement a coherent and strategic approach to teacher development. Although the book seeks to provide ideas for practicing teachers, particularly those relatively new to language teaching, we hope that experienced teachers, teacher trainers, and supervisors will find much to interest them as well. In recent years, language teachers in many parts of the world have expressed a growing interest in their own professional development. This is seen in the worldwide interest in such activities as virtual networks for language teachers, action research, journal writing, and portfolios, and the use of these and other activities as a basis for critical reflection on teaching practices. Although a large number of articles and a smaller number of books have been published on these issues, there have been few practical introductions to the field of professional development in language teaching as a whole and the range of activities and procedures that can be used for this purpose. This book seeks to meet this need.

This book examines eleven different procedures that can be used to facilitate professional development in language teaching: workshops, self-monitoring, teacher support groups, journal writing, peer observation, teaching portfolios, analysis of critical incidents, case analysis, peer coaching, team teaching, and action research. In addition, the opening chapter presents an overview of the nature of professional development and provides a conceptual framework for the book as a whole.

Each chapter examines, in a straightforward and nontechnical way, one approach to teacher development in language teaching. The goals of each activity are discussed, the methodology of using it, advantages and problems associated with it, and practical examples (in the form of *vignettes* with questions) provided of how teachers in different parts of the world have applied the activity in their own classrooms. The vignettes were obtained through our own contacts with teachers and as a response to invitations on the Internet and at workshops and seminars. The teachers' own names are used, except where anonymity was requested. Reflection questions at the end of each vignette allow readers to consider how to apply the approach in their own teaching contexts and serve as possible topics for investigation. The goal is to help teachers and those responsible for the professional development of teachers to choose activities most relevant to their needs and to familiarize themselves with familiar as well as less familiar approaches to teacher development.

This book reflects our own approaches to teacher learning in language teaching and draws on our combined experience in North America and the Asia Pacific region. We would like to thank the teachers who responded to our requests for examples, to several anonymous reviewers for valuable feedback, and to our editor, Angela Castro, whose suggestions assisted greatly in preparing the manuscript for publication.

Jack C. Richards

Thomas S. C. Farrell

1 The nature of teacher education

This book is about how teachers can continue with their professional development as language teachers once their period of formal training is over. It also examines how supervisors and administrators can provide opportunities for such development to take place. The need for ongoing teacher education has been a recurring theme in language teaching circles in recent years and has been given renewed focus as a result of the emergence of teacher-led initiatives such as action research, reflective teaching, and team teaching. Opportunities for in-service training are crucial to the long-term development of teachers as well as for the long-term success of the programs in which they work. The need for ongoing renewal of professional skills and knowledge is not a reflection of inadequate training but simply a response to the fact that not everything teachers need to know can be provided at preservice level, as well as the fact that the knowledge base of teaching constantly changes. The following vignette is an example that shows the approach a teacher in Korea is taking to manage his own professional development.

Vignette
After teaching in Asia for 2 years without any qualifications and no teaching attributes beyond rough reflection (why didn't that lesson work?), I did the RSA CTEFLA in England (I'm an American). The course was frustrating because so much of what was taught seemed Eurocentric, with little relevance to teaching EFL in Asia. But it gave me tools and reference points for class reflection, and started me off with independent reading. Seven years later, I have begun a master's course in teaching foreign languages. It was the intervening time, however, that provided my principal opportunities for professional development. I am an active member of several TEFL societies: Attending conference sessions and reading newsletters and journals provides insights into the actions and thoughts of my contemporaries. I read professional materials regularly, and write book reviews on a monthly basis. Although I sometimes don't study these as deeply as a graduate student

would, the presentation of new ideas and the opportunity to balance them against conference presentations, newsletter articles, and regular chats with my colleagues allow theory and practice to find meaning in my own lesson planning. On the other hand, most of the planned staff development sessions I have attended have been of little relevance to the classroom. I would do better to use this time to reflect more carefully on the lessons of the past week. My aim for the next few months is to get in the habit of keeping a reflective journal, and reviewing and analyzing those entries every month or two. Unfortunately, although there have been many papers arguing the merits of reflective journals, there is little to teach how to analyze them. I have more research to do.

Robert Dickey

Reflection

- What are your plans for your professional development in the next few years?
- What kinds of organized staff-development activities have you found most useful?

As this example illustrates, teachers have different needs at different times during their careers, and the needs of the schools and institutions in which they work also change over time. The pressure for teachers to update their knowledge in areas such as curriculum trends, second language acquisition research, composition theory and practice, technology, or assessment is intense, and it is the school and the classroom that provide a major source for further professional development.

The teacher-education activities discussed in this book are based on the following assumptions:

- In any school or educational institution, there are teachers with different levels of experience, knowledge, skill, and expertise. Mutual sharing of knowledge and experience is a valuable source of professional growth.
- Teachers are generally motivated to continue their professional development once they begin their careers.
- Knowledge about language teaching and learning is in a tentative and incomplete state, and teachers need regular opportunities to update their professional knowledge.
- Classrooms are not only places where students learn—they are also places where teachers can learn.

- Teachers can play an active role in their own professional development.
- It is the responsibility of schools and administrators to provide opportunities for continued professional education and to encourage teachers to participate in them.
- In order for such opportunities to take place, they need to be planned, supported, and rewarded.

The example above also illustrates another crucial aspect of the notion of teacher education: the fact that it is a process that takes place over time rather than an event that starts and ends with formal training or graduate education. This process can be supported both at the institutional level and through teachers' own individual efforts. Both approaches will be discussed in this book. Although the primary audience addressed is classroom teachers, the kinds of activities discussed here often depend for their success on the active cooperation of program coordinators and others within the school or institution, and this audience is addressed when appropriate.

Teacher training and teacher development

Teacher training

Two broad kinds of goals within the scope of teacher education are often identified, *training* and *development*. Training refers to activities directly focused on a teacher's present responsibilities and is typically aimed at short-term and immediate goals. Often it is seen as preparation for induction into a first teaching position or as preparation to take on a new teaching assignment or responsibility. Training involves understanding basic concepts and principles as a prerequisite for applying them to teaching and the ability to demonstrate principles and practices in the classroom. Teacher training also involves trying out new strategies in the classroom, usually with supervision, and monitoring and getting feedback from others on one's practice. The content of training is usually determined by experts and is often available in standard training formats or through prescriptions in methodology books. The following are examples of goals from a training perspective:

- Learning how to use effective strategies to open a lesson
- Adapting the textbook to match the class
- Learning how to use group activities in a lesson
- Using effective questioning techniques
- Using classroom aids and resources (e.g., video)
- Techniques for giving learners feedback on performance

An example of a large-scale training initiative was a recent 60-hour in-service training program on text-based approaches to the teaching of grammar in Singapore schools, which was a mandatory course for all teachers of English in Singapore secondary schools. The content of the course was developed by an outside provider, the University of Cambridge Local Examinations Syndicate (UCLES) in conjunction with the Singapore Ministry of Education, and the training sessions were run by three educational institutions over a period of 24 months. In this case, the training was provided to help with the implementation of a new English language curriculum, one that seeks to link the teaching of grammar to the analysis of texts.

Teacher development

Development generally refers to general growth not focused on a specific job. It serves a longer-term goal and seeks to facilitate growth of teachers' understanding of teaching and of themselves as teachers. It often involves examining different dimensions of a teacher's practice as a basis for reflective review and can hence be seen as "bottom-up."

The following are examples of goals from a development perspective:

- Understanding how the process of second language development occurs
- Understanding how our roles change according to the kind of learners we are teaching
- Understanding the kinds of decision making that occur during lessons
- Reviewing our own theories and principles of language teaching
- Developing an understanding of different styles of teaching
- Determining learners' perceptions of classroom activities

Strategies for teacher development often involve documenting different kinds of teaching practices; reflective analysis of teaching practices, examining beliefs, values, and principles; conversation with peers on core issues; and collaborating with peers on classroom projects. However, although many things can be learned about teaching through self-observation and critical reflection, many cannot, such as subject-matter knowledge, pedagogical expertise, and understanding of curriculum and materials. Professional development, therefore, should go beyond personal and individual reflection. For example, it can include exploration of new trends and theories in language teaching; familiarization with developments in subject-matter knowledge such as pedagogical grammar, composition theory, or genre theory; and critical examination of the way schools and language programs are organized and managed.

The following vignette from a young English teacher in Cambodia shows how he is trying to address both his immediate needs and his longer-term development.

Vignette

I did my BA TEFL degree in Cambodia, and taught part-time at a private institute while I was studying. After I graduated, I got a job teaching at the university and I have been teaching there now for 2 years. My part-time job was the starting point of my development as a teacher and enabled me to make connections between my university course and the classroom. Before I started teaching at the university, I worked for 2 months with some of the senior lecturers and subject coordinators to familiarize myself with the tasks I would have to carry out. Since I have been teaching at the university, I have also tried to observe other teachers and learn from them. I have also taken a computer-training course. A highlight for me was attending my first international conference, held in Phnom Penh. Now I think I appreciate the importance of research for any professional development. Staff-development activities in my department (mostly in the form of a discussion guided by a more experienced senior lecturer) have also been very useful. I also organize a speaking club for our students, which has taught me the importance of extracurricular activities in language learning. My main challenges at present are caused by having to teach large classes and the shortage of up-to-date books and resources in our library. I hope I will have the chance for further training in the future.

Chan Virak

Reflection

- How much collaboration is there among teachers in your institution? What forms does it take?
- What are some of the problems language teachers face in the first years of teaching?

Understanding teacher learning

Teacher-education processes derive their rationale from assumptions about the nature of teacher development and how it takes place. This field has been called teacher learning (Freeman & Richards, 1996) and is concerned with exploring questions such as the following: What is the nature of teacher knowledge and how is it acquired? What cognitive processes do we employ while teaching and while learning to teach? How do experienced and novice teachers differ? These questions are themselves dependent on our conceptualization of the nature of language teaching and our understanding of the knowledge, attitudes, skills, and processes we employ while teaching.

Conceptualizations of teacher learning

A number of conceptualizations of teacher learning can be found underlying recent and less recent teacher-education processes, and although such conceptualizations sometimes overlap and may be understood differently by different theoreticians, they can lead to different approaches to teacher education.

Teacher learning as skill learning

This view sees teacher learning as the development of a range of different skills or competencies, mastery of which underlies successful teaching. Teaching can be broken down into discrete skills that can be mastered one at a time. The skills targeted with this approach (e.g., questioning, giving explanations, presenting new language) are those identified with a model of effective teaching. Teacher training involves presenting and modeling the skills and providing opportunities for teachers to master them.

Teacher learning as a cognitive process

This approach views teaching as a complex cognitive activity and focuses on the nature of teachers' beliefs and thinking and how these influence their teaching and learning. It emphasizes that "teachers are active, thinking decision-makers who make instructional choices by drawing on complex practically-oriented, personalized, and context-sensitive networks of knowledge, thoughts, and beliefs" (Borg, 2003, p. 81). In teacher education, it encourages teachers to explore their own beliefs and thinking processes and to examine how these influence their classroom practice. Processes used include self-monitoring, journal writing, and analysis of critical incidents.

Teacher learning as personal construction

This educational philosophy is based on the belief that knowledge is actively constructed by learners and not passively received. Learning is seen as involving reorganization and reconstruction and it is through these processes that knowledge is internalized. New learning is fitted into the learner's personal framework (Roberts, 1998). In teacher education, this has led to an emphasis on teachers' individual and personal contributions to learning and to understanding of their classrooms, and it uses activities that focus on the development of self-awareness and personal interpretation through such activities as journal writing and self-monitoring.

Teacher learning as reflective practice

This view of learning is based on the assumption that teachers learn from experience through focused reflection on the nature and meaning of teaching experiences (Schon, 1983; Wallace, 1991; Richards & Lockhart, 1994). Reflection is viewed as the process of critical examination of experiences, a process that can lead to a better understanding of one's teaching practices and routines. In teacher education, this has led to the notion of reflective teaching, that is, teaching accompanied by collecting information on one's teaching as the basis for critical reflection, through such procedures as self-monitoring, observation, and case studies.

The teacher-development activities discussed in this book are not linked to a single theory of teacher learning because we believe that teachers can usefully learn from procedures drawn from different educational philosophies. However, the majority of the activities discussed throughout the book can be seen as reflecting a view of teacher learning as a cognitive process, as personal construction, and as reflection on action.

Novices and experts

Another important dimension of understanding what is meant by teacher development is the difference between a novice teacher and an expert teacher. Although the nature of expertise in language teaching is an underexplored research field (however, see Tsui, 2003), some of the differences between novice and experienced language teachers seem to lie in "the different ways in which they relate to their contexts of work, and hence their conceptions and understanding of teaching, which is developed in these contexts (Tsui, 2003, p. 245). Expert teachers thus exhibit differences in the way they perceive and understand what they do. Some of these differences include the following (Tsui, 2003):

- A richer and more elaborate knowledge base
- Ability to integrate and use different kinds of knowledge
- Ability to make sound intuitive judgments based on past experience

- A desire to investigate and solve a wide range of teaching problems
- A deeper understanding of students and student learning
- Awareness of instructional objectives to support teaching
- Better understanding and use of language learning strategies
- Greater awareness of the learning context
- Greater fluidity and automaticity in teaching

Experienced teachers approach their work differently from novices because they know what typical classroom activities and expected problems and solutions are like (Berliner, 1987). By comparison, novice teachers typically are less familiar with subject matter, teaching strategies, and teaching contexts and lack an adequate repertoire of "mental scripts and behavioral routines" (Berliner, 1987, p. 72).

The following vignette, from a teacher in the United States, shows not only the influence of a Master of Arts (M.A.) in teaching ESL but also the inspiration of working with expert teachers on this teacher's professional development.

Vignette

I got a Master of Arts in teaching ESL from the University of Minnesota. But more important, I worked in a variety of well-organized ESL/EFL programs right from the start of my career. I've been fortunate because I've always been in contact with people who were experts in some aspects of the field, so I've been able to have lunchtime conversations that helped keep me up to date. The most helpful things in my professional development were those informal contacts with smart people. That's how I developed my interests in vocabulary teaching, in using corpora to enhance teaching, and in writing materials. Also very helpful were courses I took in linguistic analysis and English syntax at the University of Minnesota, although the methods courses I took, which were little more than surveys of the faddish "methods" of the 1970s and 1980s, were not helpful—I have never applied any of that in my teaching life.

Larry Zwier

Reflection

- How have you been able to apply what you learned in your TESL/TEFL studies since you started teaching?

- How can teachers and schools make best use of the expertise of e
  enced teachers?

Many of the teacher-development activities discussed throughout this bo
seek to enable teachers with different levels of expertise to work together
through peer observation, team teaching, mentoring, group discussion, and
joint planning and problem solving.

Individual and institutional perspective

The individual perspective

Professional development is directed toward both the institution's goals and
the teacher's own personal goals. Achieving personal growth and improving departmental performance can go hand in hand. Most schools strive
for a mix of both. The vignettes above demonstrate that teachers are generally interested in adding to their professional knowledge and keeping up
to date with theory and practice in the field, in improving their teaching
skills so that they feel more confident about what they teach and achieve
better results with their students. They may also be interested in clarifying
and understanding their principles, beliefs, and values, as well as the nature
and values underlying the schools in which they work, so that they can be
empowered. These can all be considered as examples of teacher development from the perspective of the individual teacher. From the point of view
of the teacher's personal development, a number of areas of professional
development may be identified:

- *Subject-matter knowledge*. Increasing knowledge of the disciplinary basis of TESOL—that is, English grammar, discourse analysis, phonology,
  testing, second language acquisition research, methodology, curriculum
  development, and the other areas that define the professional knowledge
  base of language teaching
- *Pedagogical expertise*. Mastery of new areas of teaching, adding to one's
  repertoire of teaching specializations, improving ability to teach different
  skill areas to learners of different ages and backgrounds
- *Self-awareness*. Knowledge of oneself as a teacher, of one's principles
  and values, strengths and weaknesses
- *Understanding of learners*. Deepening understanding of learners, learning styles, learners' problems and difficulties, ways of making content
  more accessible to learners

- *Understanding of curriculum and materials.* Deepening one's understanding of curriculum and curriculum alternatives, use and development of instructional materials
- *Career advancement.* Acquisition of the knowledge and expertise necessary for personal advancement and promotion, including supervisory and mentoring skills

The institutional perspective

In many situations, teacher training provides adequate preparation for a teacher's initial teaching assignments during the first few years in a school. New teachers tend to have a fairly heavy teaching load and tend to get the more "basic" and less problematic courses. However, it is also generally the case that the preservice courses they took were of a fairly general nature, somewhat theoretical, and not directly relevant to their teaching assignments, and thus much of what they need to know has to be learned on the job, as is seen in the vignettes above.

After teachers have been teaching for some time, however, their knowledge and skills sometimes become outdated or there may be a lack of fit between the knowledge and skills the teacher possesses and what the school needs. For example, a teacher may have to take on more difficult tasks for which he or she has not received any formal training, such as the preparation or supervision of entrance tests; or, as a result of staff changes, the teacher may have to take on new assignments that were not previously part of his or her teaching; or a key staff member may leave and his or her teaching may have to be taken over by others, none of whom share the teacher's specialization. Qualifications too soon become outdated as a result of changes in the field.

The most practical response to this situation is for the school to provide the means by which teachers can acquire the knowledge and skills they need. Here, teacher development is primarily conceived of in terms of the needs of the institution. Because it refers to developmental activities within a school or institution, it is usually referred to as *staff development* and often takes the form of *in-service training.* It is intended to directly or indirectly enhance the performance of the institution as a whole, as well as to contribute incidentally to the teacher's individual development. Hence it has the following goals:

- *Institutional development.* Improvement of the performance of the school as a whole, that is, to make it more successful, attract more students, and achieve better learning outcomes. Most successful organizations regard the training and development of their staff as a matter of high priority.

- *Career development*. It also facilitates the professional advancement of teachers to more senior positions in the institution (e.g., senior teacher, coordinator) by providing them with the necessary knowledge and skills. Increased job satisfaction that results will lead to better teacher performance and better teacher retention.
- *Enhanced levels of student learning*. An important goal is to raise the achievement levels of students in the institution, a goal that is not only important for its own sake but that also adds to the reputation of the institution and its teachers.

From the institutional perspective, professional development activities are intended not merely to improve the performance of teachers but to benefit the school as a whole. Consequently, opportunities for professional development should be provided for all staff. A program coordinator may well need to complete a master's degree in TESOL, but a newly hired teacher may also need training in how to use video effectively as a teaching resource. Both needs are equally important because the success of a school program may well depend on both the strengths of its curriculum and the teaching skills of its junior staff. Improvement of teaching skills and acquisition of new information, theories, and understanding are not goals in themselves: They are part of the process of institutional development. The fact that a teacher has, on his or her own initiative, acquired a specialization in New Zealand literature, for example, may be commendable, but it may be irrelevant to the school's goals. Burns (1999, p. 209) argues that professional development activities such as action research that are "integrated into school or organizational change become a powerful way of facilitating school curriculum renewal and ensuring that language teachers retain greater ownership of curriculum implementation."

Joyce (1991) identifies five dimensions of institutional improvement that teacher development can contribute to:

1. *Collegiality*. Creating a culture through developing cohesive and professional relationships between staff (and the wider community), in which "broad" vision-directed improvements as well as day-to-day operations are valued
2. *Research*. Familiarizing staff with research findings on school improvement, teaching effectiveness, and so on, which can support "in-house" development
3. *Site-specific information*. Enabling and encouraging staff to collect and analyze data on students, schools, and effects of change—both as part of a formal evaluation and informally
4. *Curriculum initiatives*. Collaborating with others to introduce change in their subject areas as well as across the school curriculum

5. *Instructional initiatives*. Enabling staff to develop their teaching skills and strategies through, for example, generic teaching skills, repertoires of teaching methods, and specific teaching styles or approaches

Collaborative and self-directed learning

Collaborative learning

Although much teacher development can occur through a teacher's own personal initiative, collaboration with others both enhances individual learning and serves the collective goals of an institution. Most successful organizations depend on people working effectively together in teams, but special effort often has to be made to develop teamwork in schools because teaching is generally seen as an individual activity. The goals of collegial forms of professional development are to encourage greater interaction between teachers, peer-based learning through mentoring, and sharing skills, experience, and solutions to common problems. The school is viewed as a learning community. Collaborative professional development projects allow tasks and responsibilities to be shared. For a culture of cooperation to develop in a school, opportunities need to be provided for teachers to work and learn together through participation in group-oriented activities with shared goals, and responsibilities, involving joint problem solving. Collegiality creates new roles for teachers, such as team leader, teacher trainer, or critical friend. Cooperation becomes a value that can guide the process of teacher development. It is "grounded in the human moral and social capacity to take the position of the other through numerous forms of reciprocity, mutuality, and give and take" (Brody & Davidson, 1998, p. 6). Successful collaborative learning cannot be taken for granted, however, and must be carefully planned and monitored. The following vignette, from a teacher in the Philippines, demonstrates the crucial role collaborating with others can play in a teacher's development.

Vignette

I got my degree with a major in English from one of the best private universities in our city. But this didn't make my teaching career easy. When I started teaching, I felt so limited with the way I handled my class. I could not even identify what teaching methods I was using. I was dependent on the teacher's manual to the students' textbook and limited to teaching suggestions from some of my colleagues. I felt I wasn't really doing any justice in my teaching and I realized I needed to learn more. Having to face more than sixty students in a classroom every day forced me to read whatever I could, to experiment, and to consult others with more experience.

I was fortunate to have been sent to participate in several training seminars and workshops at local, regional, and national levels. My participation in these courses and workshops enhanced my skills and better equipped me as an English language teacher and helped me make a quick adjustment to my "baptism of fire" in the teaching profession. I was very lucky to be asked to join a team working on planning a syllabus for secondary level. I learned so much in the process. Researching and collaborating with members of the group was very enriching. From my more experienced colleagues I have learned the importance of considering students' interests and proficiency level in preparing lessons and the need to use feedback from students to make necessary adjustments in my teaching.

I know my 5-year teaching experience is not enough. I believe I still need to deepen my content knowledge and learn new methods of teaching, devote more time to working with colleagues, to examine new standards being proposed, and to seek innovative ways to improve student achievement, promote quality teaching, and motivate students. I am currently completing a diploma course in applied linguistics, which is providing many opportunities to develop, master, and reflect on new approaches to working with students.

Ali Anudin

Reflection

- What are some of the classroom realities that a university degree may not adequately prepare a teacher for?
- What do you think teachers can learn working on group projects?

Self-directed learning

An important direction in teacher development in recent years has been a movement away from "outsider" approaches to "insider" ones. The former are often based on expert knowledge as well as general theories and principles that teachers apply to their own situations; the latter are locally based approaches that encourage teachers to explore their own contexts and construct their own knowledge and understanding of what takes place in their classrooms. In self-directed learning, teachers assume responsibility for setting goals for self-development and for managing and controlling their own learning.

Among the reasons for the shift toward self-directed approaches to teacher development are a move from an authoritarian organizational structure in schools toward more democratic and participatory forms of teacher development; a shifting of responsibility for professional development from managers and supervisors to teachers themselves; and a recognition of the power of experiential and action-based learning.

Central to self-directed learning are the following processes:

- *Inquiry.* Asking questions about one's own teaching practices and seeking the information needed to answer these questions
- *Self-appraisal.* Assessing one's teaching and development on the basis of evidence from oneself and others and the ability to critically reflect and a desire to analyze oneself to determine one's strengths and weaknesses
- *Experience.* Personal experience becomes the basis and stimulus for learning.
- *Personal construction.* Meaning is personally constructed by the learner.
- *Contextualized learning.* Learning takes place in a particular context and social setting and is socially constructed.
- *Planning and managing.* Learning is dependent on the ability to set short- and long-term goals and to select strategies for their achievement.

Many of the development activities discussed in this book attribute a crucial role to self-direction.

A wide variety of methods and procedures are available for in-service teacher development, and in the remaining chapters of this book we will examine the various options available, consider what they are useful for, and describe procedures for implementing them. We will consider activities that can be carried out at the individual level, those that involve working with a colleague, those that are group-based, and those that are often a response to an institutional directive. Both the individual teacher's perspective and that of the supervisor or administrator are addressed, where appropriate. Some can be carried out in more than one mode, as Table 1 illustrates.

Table 1: *Activities for Teacher Development*

Individual	One-to-one	Group-based	Institutional
• Self-monitoring	• Peer coaching	• Case studies	• Workshops
• Journal writing	• Peer observation	• Action research	• Action research
• Critical incidents	• Critical friendships	• Journal writing	• Teacher support groups
• Teaching portfolios	• Action research	• Teacher support groups	
• Action research	• Critical incidents		
	• Team teaching		

Implementing professional development: The teacher's perspective

Teachers can plan many aspects of their own professional development. Most of the activities and procedures discussed in this book can be carried out under the teacher's own initiative, although the institution can and should play an important role in facilitating the individual initiatives of its teachers. The following guidelines reflect the teacher's perspective:

Decide what you would like to learn about your teaching and about the field

Even though you have probably completed your formal preparations as a teacher, your professional development does not stop once you have acquired your professional qualifications. The first step in planning for your ongoing professional development is to determine what your short-term and long-term goals are. These could include goals such as the following:

- To become better informed about the field
- To learn more about learning strategies and to explore ways of incorporating a focus on strategies into my teaching
- To develop more effective ways of assessing students
- To improve aspects of my teaching that are in need of review
- To develop a better understanding of English grammar and how to teach it
- To work on collaborative materials-development projects with colleagues
- To learn how to plan and evaluate a language course

The starting point is thus to focus on particular issues that seem to be important to your teaching and that you would like to know more about.

Identify a strategy to explore the topic you are interested in

This book will introduce you to a number of different ways of facilitating professional development. Which of the activities seems to be best suited to clarifying the issues you want to explore and helping you achieve your goals? We recommend starting with a simple activity, such as self-monitoring or peer observation, in order to develop some preliminary ideas about the topic you are interested in. Later you can decide if you want to follow up your initial investigation with other activities, such as peer coaching or action research.

Talk to people who have taken part in a professional development activity

Try to meet and talk to teachers who have taken part in teacher-development activities of the kind you wish to try out. The Internet is an excellent way of getting in touch with teachers who share your interests and concerns. In your conversations with other teachers and with Internet colleagues, you can find out what their experience of different activities such as journal writing or team teaching was like, how they went about it, what they learned from it, and what recommendations they would give to someone who wished to carry out a similar activity.

Decide what kind of support you will need

Many of the activities discussed in this book do not need support from a coordinator or manager. However, some such as peer observation, team teaching, and peer coaching, will benefit from institutional assistance. In this case, discuss the goals of such an activity with colleagues and negotiate suitable support where available.

Select a colleague or colleagues to work with

You may want to work with a colleague or colleagues (in your own organization or from outside) in order to help you implement a teacher-development strategy or activity. You will need to find a colleague you can trust to work with you as you investigate the issue. This relationship can be in the form of a critical friendship, team teaching, peer coaching, or a teacher support group.

Set realistic goals and establish a time frame

It is important not to underestimate the time commitment that the activity you have selected may require. You are the best judge of how much time you can afford to devote to journal writing, team teaching, a discussion group, and so on. And in planning an activity you should decide on when you feel it will have achieved its aims. How many times will your support group meet? How often will you take time to write a teaching journal? How often will you and a colleague plan to observe each other's teaching? Often, the first time you carry out a particular activity should be regarded as a tryout in order for you to judge whether the activity will need to be fine-tuned or modified in light of your experience.

Evaluate what you have learned and share the results with others

Once you have carried out an activity, such as team teaching, a journal, a case study, or assembled a portfolio, step back and review what you learned from the process and whether the process could have been improved or modified in any way. How can you share what you learned with colleagues? (See the discussion above.)

Implementing professional development: The institutional perspective

From what has been said thus far, it follows that professional development, either from the perspective of the individual teacher or from that of the institution, should not be left to chance. The following guidelines reflect the institution's role in implementing a professional development program for its teachers.

Determining the needs of both the institution and its teachers

A strategic approach to professional development starts with needs analysis. Needs analysis here refers to both the institution's needs and the perceived needs of teachers. The former may be the judgment of senior teachers and management, while the latter may be determined informally through conversation with teachers or formally through administering a questionnaire or collecting information in other ways (e.g., at a staff meeting). For the institution, appraisal is often used as a way of identifying the professional development needs of teachers. This process can be facilitated either by managers/mentors or by teachers themselves as part of a process of reflective review of their needs and interests.

Needs analysis should include the needs of both the individual and the institution as a whole. At the individual level, areas for training and development for different teachers in a program can be identified and strategies recommended for helping them achieve their goals. For example, it may be found that the school needs a specialist in computer-assisted language learning, teaching young children, or teaching business English, and, if additional staff are not to be hired to address these needs, opportunities for existing staff to acquire the necessary knowledge and skills will have to be provided for.

However, in determining the needs of an institution it should be realized that research on professional development emphasizes the importance of horizontal decision making in determining goals (Sparks, 2002). Diaz Maggioli (2003, p. 4) observes: "Programs which involve participants in the planning, organization, management, delivery and evaluation of all actions in which they are expected to participate have more chances of success than those planned using a top-down approach, where administrators make decisions in lieu of teachers."

Setting goals for professional development

Information obtained from needs analysis forms the basis of setting both institutional and individual professional development goals. Both long-term and immediate goals should be identified. At times there may be differences in perceptions between institutional needs and teachers' individual interests. Eraut (1995, p. 250) suggests that in planning teacher-development activities:

- Change should be managed and phased so as not to put impossible demands on a person at any time. Teacher development also needs to be planned over a period of time to keep its demands at a realistic level.
- Each professional development activity has to be resourced and supported at a level that gives it a reasonable chance of achieving its purpose. Distributing resources over too many separate activities is likely to result in none of them being effective.
- Negotiation should take place, preferably with each individual teacher, about the proper balance between the teacher's personal needs and the needs of the school. A teacher's professional development plan should normally incorporate elements of both.

Selecting the participants

As already noted, and as will be illustrated throughout this book, professional development activities may be undertaken as either individual or collaborative projects. Careful consideration needs to be given to determine an appropriate mix of both kinds of activities within a school or institution. Within a school, there may already be some teachers who have developed some degree of expertise in activities such as journal writing, action research, or video-recording of lessons and who can give practical advice to colleagues wishing to undertake these activities for the first time. In the case of group activities, procedures for deciding on group or team membership will need to be worked out. In one school, at the beginning of the year the principal first circulated a list of different types of professional activities that teachers might like to consider. Teachers indicated their interest in particular activities and their reasons for wishing to take part in them. This information was used in setting up preliminary plans for participating teachers.

Important considerations

Cooper and Boyd (1998, pp. 58–59) suggest that traditional models of staff development often ignore principles of adult learning, such as that with adults development is linked to their self-worth and efficacy, they learn through active involvement, learning must connect with their current understanding, and that it is a continual process of identity formation and re-formation. Principles that should be reflected in a teacher development program are therefore:

1. Opportunities to try out new practice and be self-directed in the learning process
2. Careful and continuous guided reflection and discussion about proposed changes, and time to analyze one's own experience, because experience is the richest source of adult learning
3. Personal support for participants during the change process
4. Provisions for differences in style, time, and pace of learning

A wide variety of methods and procedures are available for in-service teacher development, and the goal of this book is to examine the various options available, consider what they are useful for, and describe procedures for implementing them.

Providing support

In order to carry out professional development activities, support is crucial. This will include institutional support as well as peer support and may take many different forms. For example:

- Providing information in the form of a dossier of articles or reports that make available examples and guidelines for carrying out different kinds of activities (which is the primary goal of this book)
- Providing a forum for teachers to meet and review their progress
- Arranging visits to other schools, where appropriate, to find out how activities were conducted and supported there

- Providing time for ongoing review and feedback about how well activities are working

Diaz Maggioli (2003, p. 5) observes that "the true impact of professional development comes about when efforts are sustained over time, and when support structures exist that allow participants to receive modeling and advice from more experienced peers."

Evaluating what has been learned

Once an activity has been carried out, it is important to review how well it worked and what was learned from it, and to share the findings with others and decide if it is something that would be worth recommending to others. Issues that need to be addressed include the following:

- *Describing*. Reporting on what happened, within what time frame, using what resources, and what problems occurred
- *Justifying*. Showing that something useful was accomplished from the activity
- *Improving*. Suggesting how the activity could be improved or more widely applied

Kirkpatrick (1988) suggests that the evaluation of an organization's training and development activities can be assessed at four levels:

- *Reaction*. How do people feel during and immediately after the experience?
- *Learning*. How much have they learned in terms of knowledge, skills, and attitudes?
- *Performance*. What are they doing differently now as a result of the learning experience?
- *Organizational results*. What additional benefits has the organization gained?

Brock, Yu, and Wong (1992) evaluated their learning experience at the levels of *reaction* and *learning* and confirmed the importance of review of professional development activities. They participated in a collaborative journal-writing activity, and although their overall evaluation of the experience was positive, they also emphasized that it was time-consuming and a burden at times. They concluded that the experience could have been less demanding if they had developed a tighter focus for their writing, narrowing their focus to a few salient issues rather than trying to follow too many issues at the same time.

Disseminating the results

In order to strengthen the collaborative benefits of professional development activities, avenues need to be identified for sharing the results of such inquiry with others. Because the primary audience for the results is the participating teachers and colleagues within the institution, school-based networks are an ideal forum for presenting the results. There are many options available for disseminating the results. These include:

- A brief written report of the project, which can be made available to anyone interested (such a document helps other teachers assess the feasibility and usefulness of carrying out a similar activity in their own classroom)
- A lunchtime or other form of presentation to colleagues
- An account of the project in a newsletter or e-mail forum
- A presentation at a conference
- An account of the activity in a professional magazine or journal
- A workshop exploring issues in carrying out development activities

References and further reading

Berliner, D. C. (1987). Ways of thinking about students and classrooms by more and less experienced teachers. In J. Calderhead (Ed.), *Exploring teachers' thinking* (pp. 60–83). London: Cassell.

Borg, S. (2003). Teacher cognition in language teaching: A review of research on what language teachers think, know, believe, and do. *Language Teaching*, 36(2), pp. 81–109.

Brock, M., Yu, B., & Wong, M. (1992). Journaling together: Collaborative diary-keeping and teacher development. In J. Flowerdew, M. Brock, & S. Hsia (Eds.), *Perspectives on second language teacher education* (pp. 295–307). Hong Kong: City Polytechnic of Hong Kong.

Brody, C. M., & Davidson, N. (Eds.). (1998). *Professional development for cooperative learning: Issues and approaches*. New York: State University of New York Press.

Burns, A. (1999). *Collaborative action research for English language teachers*. New York: Cambridge University Press.

Cooper, C., & Boyd, J. (1998). Creating sustained professional growth through collaborative reflection. In Brody & Davidson, pp. 26–49.

Crandall, J. A. (2000). Language teacher education. *Annual Review of Applied Linguistics,* 20, pp. 34–55.

Diaz Maggioli, G. (2003). Fulfilling the promise of professional development. *IATEFL Issues* (August–September), pp. 4–5.

Eraut, M. (1995). Developing professional knowledge within a client-centered orientation. In Guskey & Huberman, pp. 227–252.

Freeman, D. (1982). Observing teachers: Three approaches to in-service training and development. *TESOL Quarterly,* 16(1), pp. 21–28.

Freeman, D., & Richards, J. C. (Eds.). (1996). *Teacher learning in language teaching.* New York: Cambridge University Press.

Glover, D., & Law, S. (1996). *Managing professional development in education.* London: Kogan Page.

Green, G. (2002). *Training and development.* Oxford: Capstone Publishing.

Guntermann, G. (Ed.). (1993). *Developing language teachers for a changing world.* Lincolnwood, IL: National Textbook Company.

Guskey, T. R., & Huberman, M. (Eds.). (1995). *Professional development in education.* New York: Teacher's College, Columbia University.

Head, K. & Taylor, P. (1997). *Readings in teacher development.* Oxford: Heinemann.

Joyce, B. (1991). The doors to school improvement. *Educational leadership,* 48, p. 8.

Kirkpatrick, D. L. (1988). *Evaluating training programs: The four levels.* San Francisco: Berret-Koehler.

Richards, J. C., Li, B., & Tang, A. (1998). Exploring pedagogical reasoning skills. In J. C. Richards, *Beyond training* (pp. 86–102). New York: Cambridge University Press.

Richards, J. C., & Lockhart, C. (1994). *Reflective teaching in second language classrooms.* New York: Cambridge University Press.

Roberts, J. (1998). *Language teacher education.* London: Arnold.

Rolheiser, C., & Stevahn, L. (1998). The role of staff developers in promoting effective decision-making. In Brody & Davidson, pp. 50–62.

Schon, D. A. (1983). *The reflective practitioner.* New York: Basic Books.

Sparks, D. (2002). *Designing powerful staff development for teachers and principals.* Oxford: National Staff Development Council.

Tjepkema, S., & Wognum, A. A. A. (1999). Human resource development in a corporate setting from an organizational point of view. In A. Visscher (Ed.), *Managing schools towards higher performance* (pp. 245–285). Lisse (Netherlands): Swets and Zeitlinger.

Tsui, A. B. M. (2003). *Understanding expertise in teaching: Case studies of ESL teachers.* New York: Cambridge University Press.

Wallace, M. (1991). *Training foreign language teachers: A reflective approach.* Cambridge: Cambridge University Press.

2 Workshops

Many of the activities discussed in this book may be unfamiliar to teachers or require some degree of planning if they are to be successfully implemented. In our experience, a workshop is often the best way of exploring what a particular professional activity, such as action research, consists of, what its pros and cons are, and whether it might be of interest to teachers. Workshops, however, are often hit-or-miss affairs and are sometimes thrown together without a great deal of preliminary thought or planning. In view of the important role workshops can have in preparing teachers for different kinds of professional development initiatives, in this chapter we will examine the nature of workshops and suggest ways in which they can be used to support some of the activities we discuss throughout the book.

What are workshops?

A workshop is an intensive, short-term learning activity that is designed to provide an opportunity to acquire specific knowledge and skills. In a workshop, participants are expected to learn something that they can later apply in the classroom and to get hands-on experience with the topic, such as developing procedures for classroom observation or conducting action research. Workshops can also provide opportunities for participants to examine their beliefs or perspectives on teaching and learning, and use this process to reflect on their own teaching practices. Workshops can address issues related to both institutional improvement and individual development and they are led by a person who is considered an expert and who has relevant experience in the workshop topic. In our experience, workshop-based learning is particularly suitable for teachers because workshops can be scheduled outside of class time (e.g., on a Saturday). Workshops are one of the most common and useful forms of professional development activities for teachers (Richards, Gallo, & Renandya, 2001), although the first workshop for teachers dates back only to 1936 (O'Rourke & Burton, 1975). The following vignette briefly outlines how one teacher decided to attend a workshop.

Vignette

Recently I attended a workshop on doing research in your own classroom. I thought this sounded interesting because I plan to do a master's degree some time and I thought this might help me prepare for it. However, I was also worried that it might be somewhat technical and not very practical. I was agreeably surprised, however, and the workshop leader had an interesting approach to the workshop. We worked mostly in small groups and spent the first hour identifying issues that we could research in our own classrooms. Then we considered different ways of collecting and analyzing data, working on some case studies that the workshop leader had prepared. We also talked about ethical issues in doing research, something I had never considered. This was a very successful workshop for me because I came away feeling much more confident about doing classroom research. I also enjoyed meeting other teachers and sharing some of our experiences.

Eric Harmsen

Reflection

- Have you participated in successful workshops? What do you think made them successful?
- What are some issues you would like to explore in a workshop?

Workshops differ from other learning formats often used in professional development, such as seminars. A seminar is a session or series of sessions in which a group of experienced people discuss an issue and exchange information and experience. As with a workshop, a seminar is usually led by a person who is an expert in the area, but in the case of a seminar the participants may be equally experienced or as knowledgeable as the resource person. In both a seminar and a workshop all participants are expected to contribute actively, though the mode of participation differs. As the name implies, it is a place where work is accomplished, directed to the collaborative exploration and resolution of problems.

Benefits of workshops

We have found workshops to be one of the most powerful and effective forms of teacher-development activity. There are several benefits of workshop-based learning for language teachers.

- *Workshops can provide input from experts.* As was discussed in Chapter 1, self-directed professional development in language teaching (e.g., through journal writing, observation, or portfolios) can be used to learn many important things about teaching. Although not all workshops involve input from experts, teachers often need the help of an expert in order to familiarize themselves with such topics as portfolio assessment, classroom research, and alternative assessment, and a workshop can provide an opportunity for an expert in an area to share knowledge and experience with teachers in a comfortable learning environment.
- *Workshops offer teachers practical classroom applications.* A workshop is intended to enhance teachers' practical skills and help resolve problems, rather than simply improve theoretical understanding. Teachers attending a workshop should therefore come away with ideas, strategies, techniques, and materials that can be used in their classrooms.
- *Workshops can raise teachers' motivation.* Workshops take teachers out of the classroom to a forum where they can share problems and concerns with colleagues or teachers from different schools. They also can serve to rekindle teachers' enthusiasm for teaching. The concentrated nature of a workshop also helps to maintain participants' interest level.
- *Workshops develop collegiality.* Because a workshop is a highly interactive activity, spending a few hours with other colleagues helps develop bonds of collegiality and personal relationships that often last well beyond the workshop itself.
- *Workshops can support innovations.* Workshops can be a crucial strategy in the implementation of a curriculum or other kind of change. For example, if a new educational policy mandates an unfamiliar teaching or curriculum approach such as competency-based instruction or content-based instruction, workshops would be an ideal format for preparing teachers for the change.
- *Workshops are short-term.* A workshop can vary in length, though it is usually of limited duration. Because a workshop focuses on a very specific topic, it can be dealt with in a limited time frame, which is an advantage for teachers and institutions that have very little time available for additional activities.
- *Workshops are flexible in organization.* Although workshops involve consideration of issues and problems, often based around theoretical or conceptual input followed by problem solving and application in pairs or groups, the way such activities are sequenced can vary according to the preferences of the leader and the participants.

The following vignette is from a teacher who attended a workshop on group work and is about what she learned from the workshop.

Vignette

Recently I attended a workshop on managing successful group work, organized by our local teachers' association. I like to do a lot of group activities with my students, but I am never sure how successful they are or how to make them more effective. Also, I assumed that running group activities was mainly a question of common sense. However, this workshop was very useful because the leader was a specialist in cooperative learning and offered a whole new perspective on the nature of group interaction. One of the most interesting parts of the workshop was when we studied a cooperative learning technique based on the jigsaw technique, where each group mastered a text on an aspect of cooperative learning theory and then took turns presenting it to the other groups. All in all, I found the workshop very useful and I have started implementing some of the things we learned. If I were to comment negatively about the workshop, it would be that it was too crowded and we could not interact enough with the facilitator.

UnKyung Lee

Reflection

- What do you think is the optimum number of participants in a workshop?
- What kinds of issues would you expect to explore in a workshop about group work?

Procedures for planning effective workshops

We recommend the following procedures when planning workshops:

1. *Choose an appropriate topic.* Workshop-based learning is appropriate for issues that involve problem solving and the development of practical skills. We have found that it is generally less appropriate for teaching abstract theory or information without any practical application, for which a short course would be more suitable. Because a workshop is dependent on group discussion and shared perspectives, the topic should also be one that participants have relevant experience in and ideas that they can draw on, or, in cases where participants have little experience of the topic, a strong interest in learning more about it. A successful workshop topic is also likely to be one that addresses a problem that participants are experiencing or a situation they wish to change or improve. Suitable workshop topics can often be identified

through discussions with teachers or supervisors. The topic should be clearly focused, owing to the limited time frame, and should examine one or two issues in depth rather than seek to survey a vast area.

2. *Limit the number of participants.* Workshops are best suited to a limited number of participants because an effective workshop requires the facilitator to interact with participants, giving them an opportunity to present their ideas and suggestions, as well as to interact with participants and give feedback on problems and solutions. A workshop can be satisfactorily run for as few as six participants and as many as thirty. Once numbers exceed thirty, there is a danger that it will revert to a lecture-type format and lose its value as a workshop. Depending on the number of participants, a workshop is normally organized around small-group interaction. The goal is to form groups in which collectively the group members have the knowledge and experience needed to complete the tasks that have been set and there are opportunities for all members of the group to participate. If group size is too large (e.g., seven) there is a tendency for some members to be silent participants; hence four is a better size to aim for because it divides into two pairs who can work as pairs and then regroup as a foursome. Group work often requires that one member of the group be a group leader and one be a recorder. These roles can be rotated around the group during the workshop. The facilitator's job is to make sure the group keeps to the task and gets through it in the time assigned and to make sure that everyone has a chance to participate. The recorder keeps an account of the group's decisions.

3. *Identify a suitable workshop leader.* The success of a workshop is often dependent on the qualities of the workshop leader. Not everyone who is a good classroom practitioner or university lecturer is a good workshop leader. More than one workshop leader is often necessary because the nature of workshop-based learning means that it is difficult for a leader to adequately interact with more than twelve to fifteen participants. If the number of participants exceeds this, several leaders will be needed. Participants then have access to several experts or facilitators during the course of the workshop.

In order to plan and conduct a successful workshop, a number of qualities are needed in the workshop leader or leaders:

- *Knowledgeable about the subject matter.* Although a workshop builds on the experience and ideas of its participants, what they learn from it should not simply be based on the collective ideas of its members. New ideas and knowledge should also be provided through direct input from the facilitator, who should also be able to provide informed answers to questions that participants raise and arouse the participants' enthusiasm for the workshop topic.

- *Familiar with ways of conducting a workshop.* The facilitator should be skilled at facilitating group-based learning, good at time management, and able to resolve any problems that develop during the workshop.
- *Familiar with teaching adult learners.* Pitching a workshop at the right level for an audience that often includes very experienced teachers is a crucial skill. We have often observed that experienced teachers are sometimes skeptical that they have anything new to learn from a workshop. They may have many ideas but also have fixed opinions. The leader may also have to deal tactfully with participants who have strongly differing opinions. Wood, Killian, McQuarrier, and Thompson (1993, pp. 21–24) discuss several features of adult learners that are relevant to the planning of workshop-based learning. Adult learning involves the ego, and adults need concrete, direct experience where they practice what they are learning. Most adults learn more in small groups, they come to learning with a wide range of differences, they want some control over what they learn, and they are basically self-motivated. At the same time, adults need feedback and do not automatically transfer learning from training to practice.

4. *Plan an appropriate sequence of activities.* A workshop should allow ample opportunity for participants to absorb new information, participate in group discussion, discuss problems, and arrive at solutions and applications to their own classrooms. Group tasks should not necessarily require one "correct" solution but allow for solutions to be arrived at through group consensus or allow for different acceptable outcomes. Watson, Kendzior, Dashor, Rutherford, and Solomon (1998, pp. 161–162) describe the following kinds of activities used in workshops ranging from 1 day to 5 days on cooperative learning:

- *Unity-building activities.* Fun, nonthreatening, but purposeful activities designed to let participants get to know each other and share relevant ideas and experiences related to the workshop topic
- *Direct instruction presentations.* Sessions providing an overview or instruction on key topics, ideas, theories, and techniques, often supplemented by written materials
- *Partner work.* Pair-work problem-solving and discussion activities involving interviewing, problem solving, discussing readings
- *Small-group discussions.* Focus groups of four to six members in which participants discuss information and suggestions from the workshop and develop strategies for application
- *Role-play/practice sessions.* Role-play sessions in which participants apply and practice strategies and techniques presented during the workshop

- *Co-planning activities*. Lesson-planning activities designed to develop skills in working with a partner
- *Reflection time*. Sessions scheduled at the end of each day to reflect on what has been learned in pair or group discussion or through journal writing

Finding suitable resources is often crucial to the success of a workshop. These resources might include units from textbooks, lesson plans, lesson transcripts, video or audio recording of lessons or lesson segments, reference books, or samples of learner language, which participants may consult as they carry out workshop tasks.

5. *Look for opportunities for follow-up*. If a workshop is to have any impact, follow-up action is normally needed. This might consist of planning for follow-up action and establishing a timetable for things to occur. Follow-up means considering what use teachers will make of what they have learned, when they will implement their new ideas and strategies, how they will apply what they have learned to classroom teaching, and how they will monitor their efforts and share the results of their efforts.

6. *Include evaluation*. A workshop is generally evaluated in terms of both its content and the processes it employs. It can be evaluated through the use of a questionnaire and through interviews with participants. Evaluation should seek information on the following issues:

- *Design of the workshop*. Did it achieve its goals? Was the content suitable? Was the coverage of material appropriate? Was the time spent on each topic and on group work sufficient? Were the tasks effective?
- *Presenter*. Was he or she a successful facilitator and a good communicator? Was he or she knowledgeable? Were his or her teaching methods suitable for adult learners?
- *Resources*. What resources were used and were they adequate and useful (e.g., articles, books, materials)?
- *Learner participation*. Did all participants have a chance to speak? Did they stay through the workshop? What kind of interaction and participation was required of them? Was the workshop appropriate for those who attended?
- *Learner satisfaction*. Were the participants satisfied with the topics, the facilitator, their level of involvement, the facilities, the tasks, and the structure of the workshop?
- *Changes in understanding*. Did the participants develop new understandings of the content? Have they changed as a result of the workshop?
- *Usefulness and applicability*. Can the knowledge gained during the workshop be applied in teaching? Will the knowledge transfer to participants'

teaching situations? What impact is the workshop likely to have? It might be useful to ask them to identify two or three of the most important things they learned from the workshop, and how they will be able to apply them in their teaching.

The following vignette describes how workshops are set up in a university language department.

Vignette

In our department teachers are offered the chance to take part in one workshop per semester. The workshops are usually led by members of the department, though sometimes an outside specialist is invited to lead a workshop. To find topics for workshops, all teachers are consulted early in the semester for suggestions about workshop topics and to see if they would like to organize a workshop. We have a set of departmental guidelines we can use, if we wish, that give suggestions on how to run the workshop and for follow-up. Most of the teachers in our program take part in a workshop at least once a year, though workshops are not compulsory. I find they are usually helpful and are also a nice break from teaching.

Dino Mahoney

Reflection

- What topics do you think you could offer a workshop on?
- What kinds of follow-up activities can be useful after a workshop?

Summary

Workshop-based learning is such a familiar format for professional development that the nature of effective workshops is often taken for granted. The fact that many teachers have experienced both effective and less effective workshops during their careers is a reminder that a successful workshop needs to be well planned and coordinated and not thrown together at the last moment. A well-conducted workshop can have a lasting impact on its participants and workshops can plan a key role in achieving a school's institutional goals as well as meeting some of the individual needs of its teachers. Providing opportunities for senior teachers to develop skills in running workshops is an important part of staff development. Giving teachers regular opportunities to update their professional knowledge through participating in workshops also sends an important message about the school's commitment to quality and to professional development. Workshops also give teachers an opportunity to step back from the classroom, make connections with colleagues, and return to teaching with a renewed sense of enthusiasm.

Example of workshop

STETS
(Singapore Tertiary English Teachers Society)
Annual Workshop
conducted by
Dr. Thomas S. C. Farrell
29 November 2002
http://www.stets.org.sg/stetsAnnualWorkshop.htm

Reflective Practice for Language Teachers

Schedule

9:15–10:45

I. Reflective Practice: Setting the Scene/Defining Reflective Practice
   1. **Introduction** – Overview of workshop
   2. **Teaching Story** – Journal writing
   3. **Defining Reflective Practice**
      a. *Are you a reflective teacher?*
      b. *Define reflective practice*
      c. *Definitions of reflective practice*
   4. **Current Levels of Reflection**
      a. *Reflective practice levels attributes clarification*
      b. *Five features of a reflective teacher*

10:45 Tea break

II. Critical Incidents – Who Are You as a Language Teacher?

11:15–12:45

   1. **The "Tree of Life"**
   2. **Teachers' Beliefs**
   3. **Reflecting about Two Different Classes**

12:45 Lunch

III. Reflective Practice: Conceptions of Language Teaching;
Generating Topics

13:45–15:15

1. **Methods**
   a. *Classroom observation (video viewing)*
   b. *Journal writing*
   c. *Group discussions*
2. **Generating Topics for Reflection – Groups**

15:15 Tea break

IV. Reflective Practice: Providing Opportunities for Language
Teachers to Reflect/Teaching

15:45–17:15

1. **Teaching Portfolios: Compiling Teaching Portfolios for Reflection**
2. **Dewey's Reflective Disposition**
3. **Conclusion:** The facilitator welcomes questions, comments, and disagreements.

References and further reading

Birchak, B., Connor, C., Crawford, K. M., Kahn, L., Kaser, S., Turner, S., & Short, K. (1998). *Teacher study groups*. Urbana, IL: National Council of Teachers of English.

Fleming, J. A. (1997). New perspectives on designing and implementing effective workshops. *New Directions for Adult and Continuing Education, 76.* San Francisco: Jossey-Bass.

Lotan, R., Cohen, E., & Morphew, C. (1998). Beyond the workshop: Evidence from complex instruction. In C. M. Brody & N. Davidson (Eds.), *Professional development for cooperative learning* (pp. 123–146). New York: State University of New York Press.

O'Rourke, M., & Burton, W. (1957). *Workshops for teachers*. New York: Appleton-Century Crofts.

Richards, J. C., Gallo, P., & Renandya, W. (2001). Exploring teachers' beliefs and processes of change. *PAC Journal* 1(1), pp. 41–64.

Sork, T. J. (Ed.). (1984). *Designing and implementing effective workshops*. San Francisco: Jossey-Bass.

Watson, M., Kendzior, S., Dasho, S., Rutherford, S., & Solomon, D. (1998). A social constructivist approach to cooperative learning and staff development: Ideas from the child development project. In C. M. Brody & N. Davidson (Eds.), *Professional development for cooperative learning* (pp. 49–62). New York: State University of New York Press.

Wood, F., Killian, J., McQuarrie, F., & Thompson, S. (1993). *How to organize a school-based staff development program*. Alexandria, VA: Association for Supervision and Curriculum Development.

3 Self-monitoring

The nature of self-monitoring

A starting point in teacher development is an awareness of what the teacher's current knowledge, skills, and attitudes are and the use of such information as a basis for self-appraisal. Often in institutions a performance appraisal by a manager or supervisor provides an outsider's perspective on current level of performance, based on classroom observation, student feedback, an interview, and other sources of information. However, teachers are also often able to make such judgments themselves based on information they collect about their own teaching. Self-monitoring or self-observation is intended for this purpose and refers to activities in which information about one's teaching is documented or recorded in order to review or evaluate teaching.

Self-monitoring or self-observation refers to a systematic approach to the observation, evaluation, and management of one's own behavior in order to achieve a better understanding and control over the behavior (Armstrong & Frith, 1984; Koziol & Burns, 1985). In everyday life, people often make use of self-monitoring, such as when a person is on a diet and makes a record of everything he or she eats and drinks each day. In this chapter we will examine three approaches to self-monitoring of language lessons: *lesson reports, audio-recording a lesson*, and *video-recording a lesson*. Like other approaches to reflective teaching, self-monitoring is based on the view that in order to better understand one's teaching and one's own strengths and weaknesses as a teacher, it is necessary to collect information about teaching behavior and practices objectively and systematically and to use this information as a basis for making decisions about whether there is anything that should be changed. In the following vignette, a language teacher in Singapore describes how he uses this process in his teaching.

Vignette

I'm currently teaching oral presentation skills to a group of intermediate-level EFL learners from different countries. I haven't been able to find any published material that matches the particular needs of the group and the particular focus of my lessons, so I'm preparing my own. Based on the information I had to go on (the professional profiles of the students, their precourse test results, learning needs analysis data, and so on), I prepared quite a few sessions in advance of the course. I'm finding that some are perfectly usable, while others need major overhaul.

At the end of each lesson I try and sit down and do a bit of recall, using the handouts as the stimulus. I ask myself questions like:

- At what stages did the students need more support?
- At what stages did I seriously overestimate or underestimate their knowledge and skills?
- Was there too much input and not enough practice or too much unproductive practice and not enough focused input?

These broad questions usually lead to microlevel considerations of timing, staging, task design, choice of vocabulary in the examples, and so on. I tend to write notes directly on a copy of the material and, assuming I teach another course like this with a similar group of students, I file it and use it as a reference for next time.

The next step is to look ahead and see if the issues that have come out of the self-evaluation of this lesson apply to material for upcoming lessons, which usually haven't yet "gone to print." I might decide that I need to include or omit whole stages or individual activities or that the pitch is too low or too high. As the course goes along, of course, I'm getting a clearer idea of what teaching/learning activities the class seems to find useful or otherwise, and this has resulted in some major changes to the material I wrote before meeting the group.

Neil England

Reflection

- What are the advantages of the procedures Neil uses?
- Why do you think teaching materials that work well with one group of students sometimes do not work well with another group of seemingly similar students?

Often when one monitors one's teaching, the information obtained is private and not necessarily shared with others. It may be part of the process by which the teacher explores aspects of his or her teaching over time. However, there may also be times when the information collected through self-monitoring is usefully shared with others. For example, sometimes we have arranged for a teacher to negotiate a series of self-monitored lessons with a mentor or supervisor and then for both to discuss the reports. Or a teacher may decide to monitor aspects of lessons with a group of colleagues and meet regularly to share the information collected.

Purpose and benefits of self-monitoring

We believe that self-monitoring offers several benefits. It allows the teacher to make a record of teaching that he or she can use for a variety of purposes, as we will discuss in this chapter. It can also provide an objective account of one's teaching. Although teachers usually feel that they have a good understanding of how they approach their teaching and the kind of teacher they are, when given a chance to review a video recording or a transcript of a lesson, they are often surprised, and sometimes even shocked, at the gap between their subjective perceptions and "objective" reality. For example, the teacher may not realize that explanations are not always very clear, that sometimes things are overexplained, that the teacher talks too quickly at times, that many students do not pay attention during the lesson, or that the teacher tends to dominate the lesson and not give students sufficient opportunity to participate. Teachers may also be unaware that they tend to speak to some students more often than others or that they have some irritating speech mannerisms, such as overfrequent use of "Yes," "Uh-huh," or "Right." The following vignette shows how a language teacher in Brazil used video analysis to monitor his correction of errors in his class.

Vignette
I mainly teach intermediate-level students in a private institute. Recently, I was interested in finding out what my response to students' errors was, so I arranged to have two of my classes videotaped. I later looked over the videos to see whether there were any patterns to my error correction. The first thing that surprised me was that I ignored about 80% of the errors students made. I also found that I tended to correct during controlled practice activities but

hardly at all during more open-ended fluency-type activities, such as when students were taking part in group discussions. I discovered that the usual strategy I employed to correct a student was simply to interrupt and provide the correct word or grammatical form. But about half the time I did that, the student did not repeat the correct form or try to correct the error.

Sergio Gonzalez

Reflection

- Have you ever videotaped your classes? If so, what were the positive and negative aspects of using a video to monitor your lessons?
- Sergio used the video to monitor his error correction strategies. If you used a video, what topic or topics would you like to self-monitor?

This example illustrates how self-monitoring can help teachers better understand their own instructional practices and make decisions about practices they are not aware of and might wish to change. It can help teachers develop a more reflective view of teaching, that is, to move from a level where they are guided largely by impulse, intuition, or routine to a level where actions are guided by reflection and self-awareness.

Another advantage to self-monitoring is that it is teacher-initiated. Self-monitoring activities are things a teacher can do in the privacy of his or her own classroom and the information collected does not need to be shared with others. Self-monitoring thus shifts the responsibility for initiating improvement in teaching practices (if improvements are necessary) from an outsider, such as a supervisor, to the teacher. It enables the teacher to arrive at his or her own judgments as to what works well and what does not work so well in the classroom. In the following vignette, an experienced EFL teacher in Japan describes her approach (writing a teaching journal) to self-monitoring.

Vignette

I first experienced self-monitoring while I was doing my teacher training. I have continued to write lesson evaluations during my 15 years as a teacher. At the start I did it to remember what had gone on, especially while getting to know students. Often, writing about a lesson was a tool for exploring things that hadn't been very successful. The process of writing helped to clarify possible ways to change my approach to the class. More recently, a colleague suggested I focus on success, writing about things that went well and trying to account for them. That was a delightful idea for me. Now I write about both "problem" lessons and successful ones.

Ellen Head

Reflection

- Why do you think writing about a teaching problem might help you find a solution to the problem?
- What can you learn through writing about a successful lesson?

Procedures used in self-monitoring

We have used the following procedures for self-monitoring.

Lesson reports

A lesson report can be thought of as the opposite of a lesson plan. Whereas a lesson plan describes what the teacher sets out to achieve in a lesson, a lesson report tries to record what actually happened during the lesson. It is normally completed shortly after a lesson has been taught and records as many important details as the teacher can remember. Obviously, some aspects of a lesson cannot be accurately recalled, such as the number of times students used a particular item of language or the variety of question types the teacher used during the lesson, but some aspects can often be recalled with a high degree of accuracy. For example, these include the following:

- The extent to which activities and materials were relatively successful or not
- Departures the teacher made from the lesson plan
- The sequence of activities used during the lesson
- Difficulties learners experienced with different parts of the lesson
- Aspects of the lesson that the teacher felt were particularly successful
- Words, expressions, or grammatical items that students needed in order to better cope with the lesson

A lesson report serves as a way of documenting such observations as a source of future learning. It may include evaluation of the lesson, but need not do so. A lesson report without evaluation serves as documentation about the lesson. When a lesson report includes evaluation, the focus is on questions such as the following:

- What aspects of the lesson worked well?
- What aspects of the lesson did not work particularly well? Why?
- What aspects of the lesson should be done differently next time?

Lesson reports can be carried out as a written narrative account of a lesson, or using a checklist or questionnaire.

WRITTEN NARRATIVE

A written narrative account of a lesson, as the name suggests, consists of a descriptive summary of the lesson. Some time after the lesson has been completed, the teacher writes a report of what happened in the lesson. The report can be both descriptive and reflective. In the descriptive part, a summary is made of what happened during the lesson without commenting on or evaluating what happened. This part of the narrative serves as a report rather than an evaluation. In the reflective part of the narrative, the teacher critically reviews what happened and comments on what could be improved or what can be learned from the lesson. The length of the narrative will depend on how much time the teacher wants to devote to it and how much detail it includes. The next vignette is an example of a narrative report of a lesson written by a language teacher.

Vignette

I teach a course called English for International Communication for officials from the Indochina countries. Yesterday, we began the next unit in the course, the theme of which is "Business." As a warm-up to the topic, the students (five each from Cambodia, Laos, and Vietnam) were to compare the effects of recent economic reforms in the three countries on the foreign investment climate in each place. Because some of the students are more familiar with this topic than others, I separated them by country so that they could (*a*) have time to think about a complex topic, (*b*) help each other come up with the language required for the discussion, and (*c*) agree on the information they would share with the others about the situation in their country. I monitored the three groups and supported them where necessary. Each student took his or her own notes on the discussion. The whole activity lasted about 20 minutes. Today, the students were mixed into five groups of three, so that each group would contain one student from each of the three countries represented in the class, and they exchanged their views based on the notes they had made the previous day. The discussion lasted for about 30 minutes, after which we came together as a whole class again to summarize the students' answers to the discussion question and provide a final opportunity for student questions and/or teacher feedback. This lasted about 15 minutes.

Evaluation

Things that worked well

On the positive side, most of the students seemed able and willing to share information about the topic with their classmates, having prepared for it the day before. Some of the discussions were rather animated. The "information gap" was real and relevant. I feel yesterday's group discussion successfully helped prepare those who are less knowledgeable about the topic to contribute to today's discussion and not feel at a loss in terms of either ideas or language, and it also helped boost the confidence of those with "expertise" in the topic area. There was a lot of cooperative learning. I was happy with the way I had grouped the students, balancing gender, background knowledge of the topic, language proficiency, and group-work skills, as well as nationality. Finally, all of the students gained new information about their neighboring countries.

Things that did not work well

I had forgotten to arrange the student groups beforehand in order to balance the countries, language abilities, personalities, and background knowledge of the students. As a result, several minutes were wasted while I did this in class. Next time I'll be better prepared! A couple of the students were not very interested in or informed about the topic (which I have no control over) and, therefore, were less participatory, but I'm not sure how to make it more interesting for them.

Randall Wolansky

Reflection

- What do you think are the characteristics of effective group work?
- What do you think could be done about the students who were less interested in the topic?

There are both advantages and disadvantages to a written narrative account of a lesson such as the one above. An advantage is that it can be structured in any way the teacher chooses. For example, it could be in note form or in a more carefully composed form. In addition, the mere act of sitting down and writing about a lesson often triggers insights into aspects of the lesson that the teacher may not have had time to consider during the lesson itself. The *process* of writing thus serves as a learning heuristic. A disadvantage of a narrative account is that it may take time to complete and that it is by nature subjective and impressionistic and may not address some important aspects of the lesson.

CHECKLISTS AND QUESTIONNAIRES

A checklist or questionnaire provides another way of documenting what happened during a lesson. Checklists or questionnaires can be developed to cover the overall structure of a lesson or to focus on particular aspects of a lesson, depending on the teacher's interests. For example, a checklist that covers the overall structure of a lesson might include items related to the lesson opening and closing, the main activities of the lesson, the amount of time spent on teacher-led activities and group activities, and the amount of time spent on different skills (e.g., speaking, listening, writing).

A checklist that focused on one aspect of the lesson, such as pronunciation, might include items related to the amount of time spent on pronunciation work, the kind of pronunciation activities in the lesson, and pronunciation difficulties that were identified.

We have found that questionnaires are often best developed collaboratively by a group of teachers who are interested in monitoring their teaching of a course in order to review and share their findings. The following checklist was developed by two teachers who wanted to monitor how they dealt with pronunciation during a course they were teaching on speaking skills.

1. Main pronunciation problems observed during the lesson:
2. Amount of time spent on pronunciation during the lesson:
3. Aspects of pronunciation addressed:
   - Individual sounds:
   - Stress:
   - Rhythm:
   - Intonation:
   - Blending:
   - Other:
4. Types of pronunciation activities used:
   - Drills:
   - Dialogues:
   - Reading aloud:
   - Other:
5. Main problems students had with these activities:
6. Effectiveness of the activities used:
7. Other ways that pronunciation could be treated:

Teachers in some situations have published their checklists for use (e.g., Pak, 1987). However, in most cases, it is necessary to adapt a published checklist to suit the specific type of class a teacher is monitoring.

In our experience, checklists or questionnaires can be completed fairly quickly and they provide a more detailed account of a lesson than might appear in a written narrative. However, checklists or questionnaires need to be carefully prepared and piloted once or twice to ensure that they capture the most important features of the lesson.

Audio-recording a lesson

Making an audio recording of a lesson is another simple approach to self-monitoring. The purpose of making a recording of a lesson is to identify aspects of one's teaching that can only be identified through real-time recording. Teachers do not often have the opportunity to hear or see themselves teach. Although teachers tend to assume that they have a fairly high level of self-awareness of their own teaching style or approach, we have found when they listen to an audio or video recording of one of their lessons, comments such as the following are not untypical:

- I didn't realize I have the annoying habit of saying "Is that right?" all the time.
- I seem to speak far too quickly a lot of the time. No wonder students have difficulty understanding me.
- I don't give the students much of a chance to speak. I need to do less talking.

McKern (cited in Burns, 1999) lists a number of questions that can be explored through both audio- and video-recording:

1. What do you wish to observe (e.g., aspects of behavior, problems)?
2. What are the positive features of the performance?
3. Are the goals of the lesson clear?
4. What is the role of the teacher (e.g., expository, inquiry)?
5. Are the students involved and interested?
6. Who is doing the talking?
7. What types of utterances are made?
8. What types of questions are asked (convergent/divergent)?
9. What type of pupil involvement is there?
10. Is the pace right?
11. What style of classroom/pupil organization is used?
12. What negative features of this performance present themselves?

13. What nonverbal behavior is present?
14. What symbols, icons, rituals, or artifacts are observed?
15. Are the voices clear?
16. Is the language formal or informal?
17. What mannerisms are evident?
18. Do any distractions occur?
19. What things have you learned from this analysis?

MAKING THE RECORDING

An audio record of a lesson can be made in several ways. For example, a cassette recorder can be placed in a central place in the classroom, such as on the teacher's desk. This will usually provide a reasonably audible recording of the teacher's voice, providing he or she does not move out of range of the cassette recorder during the lesson. It will not generally record much of the students' contributions during the lesson, however.

A tape recorder with a portable microphone attached to the teacher's clothing can also be used. This has the advantage of recording the teacher in any location in the classroom. Additionally, two or more recorders can be used and placed in different locations, including on students' desks. This will permit some of the students' contributions to be recorded.

Clearly, the logistics of making an audio record of a lesson can be complicated, and an initial decision has to be made concerning the focus of the recording—either the teacher or the students. Both can be the focus of an audio record, but preferably at different times.

A common concern of teachers when considering audio or other kinds of recording of lessons is whether the presence of the cassette recorder and the knowledge that the lesson is being recorded will influence the dynamics of the lesson, resulting in a lesson that is not really typical or representative. This needs to be taken into account when reviewing the information collected. Freeman (1998, p. 207) gives some sensible advice concerning audiotaping lessons: check the level of background noise first, use more than one recorder for group activities, and, if the teacher plans to transcribe a lesson, anticipate about 3 to 4 hours of time to transcribe 1 hour of class time.

REVIEWING THE RECORDING

In most cases, it will be sufficient simply to listen to the recording of the lesson as many times as necessary. In some cases, it may also be useful to make a written transcript of the lesson. This could be a literal word-by-word account of the lesson, or it could be in note form, depending on the purpose. The advantage of making a written transcript of a lesson is that it provides a version that can be shared with others, if necessary. For example, if the teacher is part of a group of teachers who are interested in comparing their teaching styles, it is easier to share written accounts of lessons than to listen to each other's cassettes, which could be very time-consuming. However, making a transcript of a lesson can take a large amount of time, as already noted.

In reviewing the lesson, questions should be asked concerning the teacher's personal philosophy of teaching. These relate to the kind of teaching the teacher believes characterizes good teaching. This will depend on how the teacher views such things as his or her role in the classroom and how the teacher tries to relate to students, the kind of student-teacher and student-student interaction the teacher tries to encourage, the extent to which the teacher believes in such things as learner autonomy and learner centeredness, and the extent to which he or she favors a direct or a more indirect teaching style.

Questions such as the following can then be asked: What worked well? What did not work so well? Was anything unexpected learned? What kind of teaching characterized the lesson? Were there ample opportunities for learning and for student participation? How well did I do in relation to pacing, explanations, questions, feedback to students, and creating a positive and supportive atmosphere?

Video-recording a lesson

The best record of a lesson is a video because it provides a much more accurate and complete record than a written or audio recording. Although there are intrinsic difficulties involved in videotaping a lesson, the result is often well worth the effort. The ready availability of a wide range of easy-to-use video cameras means that videotaping lessons is now a practical possibility in many situations. In preparing to videotape a lesson, the following questions need to be considered:

1. Who will do the videotaping? There are several possibilities for videotaping the lesson. The teacher could ask a colleague or a student in the class to videotape it, a technician or other member of the school staff might agree to do it, or a video camera could be set up and simply turned on.
2. What should be included in the video? A decision will have to be made concerning what the focus of the video will be. It could be the lesson as a whole or a particular aspect of the lesson, such as teacher-student interaction, or student performance of a lesson activity. If someone is

filming the lesson for the teacher, that person will need to be properly briefed on what the teacher is looking for.

Some of the same issues discussed in relation to audio-recording of a lesson also apply to videotaping a lesson, because a video is generally more intrusive than an audiocassette. Once students and the teacher become accustomed to the fact that the lesson is being videotaped, however, the lesson often proceeds in a relatively normal manner. As with audio-recording of lessons, the video will not necessarily provide a good record of the audio dimension of a lesson. Some students' voices may not be audible, and the teacher may need to stand in a position where both the teacher and the students can be seen and heard. The following vignette is about a language teacher in Korea who used video recordings of his classes as a means of self-monitoring and self-assessment.

Vignette

I benefited from using the video for self-monitoring almost immediately. As one who teaches to the moment, I find formal lesson plans to be obsolete before the class midpoint on most occasions. By sitting with peer teachers, I could stop the video and tell what I was thinking, why I was doing as I was doing, as the class continues. Thus, I could (and can) revise the lesson plan as I go. Videos of my classes have made me aware of some bad habits that I have developed over time, and watching them helped me attempt to address these problems that I might have missed had I not videotaped my classes. For example, as a result of viewing videotapes of my classes over time, I found that I had developed a "restless pacing" pattern when I teach. As for the actual physical use of video, I realized that although learners are certainly affected by the intrusion of a camera, this can be mitigated by bringing a camera on numerous occasions, which I did. I also realize that it is important that the cameras not have an operator, so I use tripods. Another option could be to have students from this same class as camera technicians, although I have not tried this yet.

Robert Dickey

Reflection

- What aspects of a lesson would you be most interested in studying, using a video recording of a lesson?
- Do you think a video recording of a lesson can be used to assess a teacher's teaching? Why or why not?

SUGGESTIONS FOR VIDEOTAPING LESSONS

1. Set up a video camera in the classroom and leave it there during a few lessons so that students become familiar with it, but do not record.
2. Decide on a focus for a video recording (e.g., you, the students, a particular group of students) and either position the camera so that it is in a suitable place or inform the cameraperson what to focus on. Then videotape the lesson.

The following suggestions (adapted from Pak, 1987) apply to the use of video as a way of making a record of students' performance during particular tasks and in order to document students' progress throughout a course.

1. Film a typical classroom activity near the beginning of the course. This could be a pair-work task, in which students interview each other about a particular topic, or it could be a role-play activity. Each student is allotted a fixed time period for the activity (e.g., 2 minutes) and the entire class is filmed.
2. After filming, keep a record of each pair of students and where they appear on the tape, in order to provide easy access to the different students on the video.
3. Repeat the procedure several times during the course.
4. Use the video to monitor the progress of individual students throughout the course. The video can also be used in class to develop the students' awareness of their own progress as well as to show areas where improvement is needed.

Pak (1987, p. 4) lists a number of areas that can be the focus when reviewing videos of students' performance (many of which could also be used when reviewing an audiotaped lesson), such as language use (e.g., fluency, accuracy, appropriateness, register, pronunciation), interactional skills (e.g., opening/closing conversations, turn taking, initiating interruptions, changing topics), as well as general features of the lesson (e.g., student involvement in the lesson, rapport among students and between teacher and students, student talking time, main areas of difficulty).

REVIEWING THE VIDEO

A videotape of a lesson provides a very different account of a lesson than an audiotape. The audio record captures everything that one can *hear* about the lesson, but the video allows the teacher to observe how he or she interacts with the students. It provides an opportunity to observe a great deal of student-to-student interaction that one normally would not have an opportunity to notice. Freeman (1998, pp. 56–57) suggests keeping the following questions in mind when reviewing a video:

- What questions do you have about your teaching as you watch your students learning in this lesson?
- What puzzles you about what you see? What are you unsure of?
- What aspects of the students' learning do you want to better understand?
- Why do you think things are happening as they are on the tape? What speculation does this raise about students' learning and/or your teaching?
- What do you know about your teaching or their learning that you are interested in verifying?

Implementing self-monitoring

The activities discussed in this chapter are strategies that both the teacher and the course coordinator can use in order to arrive at a level of self-awareness of the strengths and weaknesses of individual teachers in an organization. The information that is obtained from self-monitoring can be used in a number of ways for both teachers and course coordinators.

- *Self-affirmation and assurance.* Teaching can be a difficult and, at times, threatening activity. Each new group of students poses challenges, as does teaching a new course or using a new set of teaching materials. Although teachers can always find things about themselves that they would like to improve, most do many things well most of the time and self-monitoring is a relatively stress-free way of determining what those things are. The results can help develop the teacher's sense of confidence and thus help reinforce a positive view of oneself as a teacher.
- *Identification of problems.* As a result of self-monitoring, a teacher might find evidence of a problem that he or she was unaware of. For example, the teacher might discover that some students do not enter into activities enthusiastically, or that students tend to shift to their native language during group work, or that students make an unacceptably high level of pronunciation errors. Once a problem has been identified, the teacher can begin to examine it in more detail and try out strategies for addressing it. This could lead to observation of other teachers' classes to see if other teachers have the same problem. It could also suggest ideas for action research (see Chapter 12).
- *Areas for improvement.* Teaching is a process of ongoing renewal and further development, and self-monitoring can help to identify areas for improvement. Once these are identified, the teacher can decide what to

do about them. For example, if a teacher observes that many students are not very motivated during lessons, he or she might consider working with another teacher in a peer-coaching relationship.

Summary

Self-monitoring a sample of one's lessons is often a good starting point in planning personal professional development, because it can be used to identify issues that might later be further explored through peer coaching, action research, or in a support group. Although teachers are sometimes skeptical at first about the benefits of self-monitoring, few remain so after experiencing it and generally feel it was well worth the effort. A useful target is to try to monitor one or two lessons every semester or every time the teacher teaches a new group of students. This may involve simply audio-recording a lesson and listening to part or all of the cassette as a kind of reality check. If a particular aspect of the lesson seems problematic, then a video recording of a subsequent lesson is often a good follow-up. The information obtained can benefit not only the individual teachers but could also be used as a component of a teacher's portfolio. An audio or video recording plus a commentary on it, for example, could be included in the portfolio.

Example of a lesson report

The following is an example of excerpts from a lesson report written by a teacher who watched her videotaped class when she was teaching EFL in South Korea. She also comments about what she realized after writing the lesson report. (Note that all the students were given English names.)

Lesson report

I videotaped myself teaching class for 20 minutes. When the class was finished, I replayed the video, made notes of what happened, and wrote a postlesson report as follows:

The class. There are fifteen students registered for this low-intermediate conversation class. The students are from different majors in the arts and the sciences, and are very motivated to learn how to speak English. This is week 7 out of an 8-week term.

Class activity report. I reviewed the directions for reading, "Snapshot," the introductory reading for the new chapter in *Interchange*. The style I use is familiar to the students as I always divide the text in half and each of the pairs of students read one half of the text aloud. At the beginning of this class, I called on the best student (Caroline) to read aloud so that I could ensure success. However, I was surprised when Caroline looked down and did not immediately answer. I waited briefly and then made the gesture I always make with this direction. Caroline looked up and answered with "Change." I wondered if she had some problems with understanding the instructions.
Total time: 2 minutes 45 seconds

LATER IN THE SAME LESSON

We discussed the comprehension questions. I said, "Caroline, would you read question number one to help us focus? Then read your answer." Caroline started to read her answer. I reminded her to read question number one only because that helped us focus. Caroline explains her answer. I help her clarify whether Oprah's most impressive achievement (the topic for discussion) is her going on a diet, or having her own TV show. I ask Jack to read question number two to help us focus. Jack starts to give his answer. I interrupt and remind Jack to read question number two first before giving his answer in order to help the class focus. I correct a mistake made by Jack by writing the mistake (the phrase he used) on the board and then correcting it by crossing out the mistake. His sentence now stands as, "Kim Dae-jung helped Korea achieve democracy." Interruption: The second late student arrives 14 minutes after the start of class. I ask Daniel to discuss question number one. When he starts to give his answer, I remind him to read the question first.
Time: 6 minutes. Total: 15 minutes

WHAT I LEARNED FROM THIS REFLECTION

From reading my lesson report, I learned that Caroline needed support with specific vocabulary. I learned that Jack does not understand the task. Jack seems to get caught up in the task and forgets the specific directions, or he feels that he must complete a larger quantity of reading. After watching the video, I was impressed by how eager Jack was to answer my questions correctly when we worked through the directions for reading the comprehension questions. I had not noticed that when doing the lesson, nor when I was writing up my notes immediately after doing the lesson before watching the video. I learned that students do work hard on producing correct language as well as giving correct information. So maybe these two things are going on in their minds when they are attempting to answer questions in an EFL class. From now on I will encourage my students to ask me a question if they do not understand so that they do not have to "suppose" too much, as Jack did. I will also continue designing interesting warm-up reviews because these give students a chance to listen again to familiar and recently learned vocabulary and structures.

Jane Hoelker

References and further reading

Armstrong, S., & Frith, G. (1984). *Practical self-monitoring for classroom use*. Springfield, IL: Charles Thomas.

Burns, A. (1999). *Collaborative action research for English language teachers*. New York: Cambridge University Press.

Casanave, C. P., & Schecter, S. R. (1997). *On becoming a language educator: Personal essays on professional development*. Mahwah, NJ: Lawrence Erlbaum.

Freeman, D. (1998). *Doing teacher research*. Boston: Heinle & Heinle.

James, P. (2001). *Teachers in action: Tasks for in-service language teacher education and development*. Cambridge: Cambridge University Press.

Koziol, S. M., & Burns, P. (1985). Using teacher self-reports for monitoring English instruction. *English Education* 17(2), pp. 113–120.

Orem, R. A. (2001). Journal writing in adult ESL: Improving practice through reflective writing. *New Directions for Adult and Continuing Education,* 90, pp. 69–77.

Pak, J. (1987). *Find out how you teach*. Adelaide: Australian Migrant Program.

Qun, W., & Nicola, S. (1998). Self-development through classroom observation: Changing perceptions in China. *English Language Teaching Journal* 52(3), pp. 205–213.

Wang, X. (2004). Encouraging self-monitoring in writing by Chinese students. *English Language Teaching Journal,* 58(3), pp. 238–245.

4 Teacher support groups

The nature of teacher support groups

In Chapter 1 we stressed the importance of collaborating with other teachers in professional development. In this chapter we will examine how teachers can set up a support group with colleagues and the goals of this form of collaboration. A teacher support group can be defined as two or more teachers collaborating to achieve either their individual or shared goals or both on the assumption that working with a group is usually more effective than working on one's own. Typically, a support group will involve a group of teachers meeting to discuss goals, concerns, problems, and experiences. The group provides a safe place where teachers can take part in such activities as collaborating on curriculum and materials development, and review, plan, and carry out activities such as peer coaching, team teaching, action research, and classroom observation. At the same time, in a support group teachers get to know their colleagues better and begin to function as a community of professionals rather than as individuals working in isolation from each other. Teacher support groups, as Lieberman and Grolnick (1998, p. 723) point out, play a major role in "providing opportunities for teachers to validate both teacher knowledge and teacher inquiry."

A support group, however, is not a staff meeting or an in-service activity such as a workshop. It should not become just another opportunity to discuss school problems and policies and personnel or administrative matters (Birchak et al., 1998). Because a support group is a voluntary activity and does not include all teachers, it is not an appropriate forum to discuss or resolve matters that affect the whole school. However, a group might generate issues that could become the focus of a staff meeting. Support groups are also referred to by other names, such as *study groups, teacher networks*, and *learning circles*. We are including all of these types of teacher structures under the rubric "teacher support groups."

Purposes and benefits of teacher support groups

Teacher support groups may serve a variety of purposes, including the following:

- *Reviewing and reflecting on teaching.* Teachers teaching the same course can meet regularly to discuss strategies and approaches, methods, and materials used, and later to evaluate the course.
- *Materials development.* Members of a group may bring in materials they use for teaching the various skills (e.g., speaking, listening, writing, and reading) and discuss them with the group. Additionally, the group can develop materials as a collaborative effort; for example, the group can prepare exercises and activities based on authentic materials for a specific skill such as reading. A mini-library of materials for group members' use can be created this way. The following vignette outlines how one group of four ESL teachers, who were teaching the same intermediate-level students in a university language center in the United States, decided that the textbook they were given by the course director was not appropriate for the students, so they decided to meet as a group to see what they could do about the text.

Vignette

My colleagues and I decided to do something about the textbook we were using. Simply put, the textbook was not working in generating discussions in class because it emphasized Western topics/themes that the students (who were all from Asia!) found difficult to understand. After our first meeting, however, we decided not to abandon the textbook completely because the students had been required to purchase it by the course director, and, besides, we thought it still had some useful language points that our students could learn. So for the next few meetings we decided we would divide the textbook into four sections so that each teacher would take the responsibility for coming up with extra materials for their section, and that we would devote one meeting to each section where the teacher would outline what he or she had come up with. These materials would be related to topics/themes of the particular chapters but would also have a bridge in them so that the Asian students could relate to the topic. Well, the whole process worked out very well and when we got a new group of students from different cultures we were able to quickly change the focus of the materials to suit our needs.

Harold Bennet

Reflection

- What do you think the group gained from this process of meeting together and discussing this issue?
- What would your method of solving this problem be?

- *Trying out new teaching strategies.* The group reviews a new teaching strategy (e.g., a collaborative learning activity such as "Jigsaw Reading"). One teacher demonstrates it to the class. Later, group members try it out in their own classes and the group meets to discuss their experiences. A series of new strategies are explored in this way.
- *Peer observation.* Group members take turns observing each other's teaching and discussing their observations during group sessions. Data collected from the observations (e.g., by audiotaping or videotaping it) can be discussed in light of the group's experience and beliefs.
- *Observe videotapes.* A group might watch a series of teacher-training videos and discuss the application of what they observe to their own teaching. The following vignette outlines how three Korean EFL teachers in different institutions in Korea decided to meet regularly to discuss their teaching after they attended a talk on teacher development by a well-known academic at an international language learning and teaching conference in Korea. They wanted to videotape their classes and then watch them together.

Vignette

As we were all teaching in Seoul, and within two or three subway stops from each school, we decided that we could observe each other teach for one whole semester. However, we had never done this before, so we had to decide who would tape the classes and how we would discuss the classes as we watched the tapes. After our initial nervousness of being taped, especially for Jaehee as she was the most inexperienced teacher, we settled down to teach our classes as we normally do and, after three rounds of classroom observations and videotaping, we met to discuss the tapes. We devoted separate meetings to discuss each set of videotapes of one teacher's class. We learned many things about our teaching as a result of the videotaping and the group discussions about our lessons that followed.

Heesoon Park

Reflection

- What do you think a group can gain most from watching videotapes of their classes with other teachers?

- What rules would the group have to come up with concerning the video-taping process?

- *Write articles*. The group can jointly write articles for publication. For example, the group can prepare articles on teaching methods that were successful for them and submit the article to a teaching magazine, as illustrated in the following example from a teacher in Hong Kong.

Vignette

I work in a university English department. Every semester teachers who are interested in joining a group sign up for a group on a topic of their choice. Recently we formed four groups of four or five teachers each who were interested in writing for publication. First, each group identified the topic they wanted to write about and the publication they were writing for. We analyzed back issues of the magazine to see the kind of articles they published and the level, style, format, and so on we should aim for. Then we brainstormed to identify topics we could write about. In our group we formed two writing teams and met several times to review drafts and give suggestions for improvement. Later, we submitted our articles for publication and several were accepted for the TESOL New Ways series.

Dino Mahoney

Reflection

- Which types of support groups might be useful in your teaching context?
- What difficulties do you anticipate in setting up a teacher support group?

- *Invite outside speakers*. The group can invite a speaker who is experienced in a particular topic that interests the group.
- *Develop research projects*. A group could develop action research projects to be carried out in their classrooms. For example, the group members could collect data on how they correct students' compositions and then share their findings.
- *Plan seminars*. Group members take turns investigating a topic of interest to the group. They then lead a group discussion of it. Group members can also make plans to attend a language conference as a group.

We suggest identifying a suitable focus for supports groups through canvassing teachers for suggestions or as part of an annual staff review. When teachers join a group, they are to some extent empowered because, as an individual, a teacher may be constrained by his or her rank within the institution's staff hierarchy. For example, a teacher might feel uncomfortable raising difficulties encountered with a course that has been developed by a course coordinator. In a group, however, a nonhierarchical structure operates and rank is put aside. If the members of a group do not put aside their rank, the group cannot develop as a whole and will not function effectively. As James (1996, p. 94) says: "The person, using the group solidarity to support others and to be supported then becomes empowered to act productively elsewhere."

We have found that there are a number of benefits to be obtained through participating in a supportive teacher support group instead of "going it alone." The following are just a few:

- *Greater awareness.* Teachers can become more aware of the complex issues involved in language teaching by sharing what they have experienced with colleagues in a group. The following vignette highlights the positive results of the group meetings for one member of a teacher support group in Thailand.

Vignette

The group helped me focus on a specific problem in my teaching and then they [the group members] all helped me to reflect on this problem by listening carefully to what I had to say and by offering suggestions about how I could increase my students' time speaking English during the class. I could not have achieved this reflecting alone. They were all very supportive.

Jinda

Reflection

- What have you come to realize about your teaching as a result of talking with other teachers?

- *Increased motivation.* As part of a group a teacher might become more motivated to participate in other professional development projects outside the support group such as making presentations at seminars and conferences.
- *Effective teaching.* Membership in a teacher support group can lead to more effective and innovative changes in teaching because of the sharing and critiquing of various individual members' approaches and teaching methods.

- *Benefits to students.* Often the group will focus on issues related to learners and learning (e.g., by discussing ways of teaching learning strategies), resulting in obvious benefits for learners.
- *Overcoming isolation.* For the most part, teachers work alone in their classrooms. Participation in a teacher support group can help to overcome this isolation and foster a sharing attitude among teachers.
- *Empowerment.* Teachers may find that they become more confident in themselves and their work as a result of belonging to a group.
- *Facilitating teacher initiatives.* Teacher support groups are for teachers and are managed by teachers. They draw on the expertise and experience of practicing teachers who want to share their experiences with their peers.

Types of teacher support groups

Teacher support groups can be formed in different ways (Birchak et al., 1998; Kirk & Walter, 1981), some of which are outlined in this section.

Topic-based groups

A group is formed to discuss a specific topic of interest, such as teaching intermediate ESL writing, teaching young learners, carrying out action research, or the group might be a response to a current issue or concern in education such as the standards movements. The latter kind of group may meet for a relatively short time once the issue has been explored and debated.

School-based groups

School-based groups are composed of different kinds of educators from within a school, such as teachers, teaching assistants, librarians, multimedia lab technicians, and supervisors, and focus on concerns in which they all have a common interest. For example, the group may seek to discuss a quality assurance policy and quality assurance procedures for their school and then move on to other issues that affect the whole school.

Job-alike groups

A group can be set up according to membership principles (e.g., composition teachers, coordinators, teachers of young children) and the group meets to discuss issues related to the specific type of teaching that they do.

Reading groups

Reading groups can be set up to read and discuss professional books and articles and to gain insights that can be applied in the group members' own classrooms.

Vignette

In our university English department we regularly use reading groups to enable us to catch up with current issues in theory and practice. Through an e-mail message board we first find out what topics teachers would like to read about and who would be interested in joining (and perhaps coordinating) a reading group. Topics such as testing, genre theory, English for specific purposes (ESP), and teacher development were identified recently. The coordinator, with the help of a subject area specialist, then put together a set of articles for us to read and discuss in regular fortnightly meetings. Group members took turns preparing discussion questions. The advantages of reading groups are: We were able to read things you might not normally have time to read. You learn a lot through discussing the readings with peers, and you get ideas for follow-up application in one's teaching.

Dino Mahoney

Reflection

- Which of the types of groups discussed so far in this section would you like to join?
- What would you most like to get out of participating in a teacher support group?

Writing groups

A group can focus on preparing articles for teachers' magazines and professional publications.

Research groups

Research groups consist of teachers who are researching topics of mutual interest such as the action research example just discussed. The group decides on an issue to investigate, collects data on the issue, and meets regularly to share and discuss findings.

Virtual groups

Virtual groups consist of a group of language teachers who communicate and "interact" on the Internet, such as TESL-L, a discussion group for English as a second language or foreign language teachers.

Teacher networks

Two types of groups can exist within what are sometimes called teacher networks: peer groups within a school and teacher groups at the district level. Peer networking can also operate outside the school and within a school district and the latter can be linked to the former group. For example, a group of teachers interested in grammar can come together within a school to decide the best ways to introduce more communicative grammar activities into the curriculum. This group can then link up with other similar groups in a school district to compare what they have done on this topic and determine if they have any resource persons available to advise each other.

Forming a teacher support group

Teacher support groups can function not only within the school but may encompass several schools or school districts as well as other organizations. The process of forming a teacher support group will depend on the goals of the group. Nevertheless, certain issues must be taken into consideration when planning a support group. These are group membership, group size, group organization, group goals, group time, group meeting place, and troubleshooting.

Group membership

Finding other teachers who wish to collaborate on a group project is a crucial step in creating a teacher support group. The first decision to be made is how to recruit group members. Recruitment may be through direct recruitment (the founder or facilitator of the group contacts other potential members), through indirect recruitment (the group founder or facilitator asks the school or a supervisor/coordinator to advertise or identify potential group members), or through other group members.

Group size

Once the membership issues have been decided, the issue of group size becomes important. Kirk and Walter (1981) suggest that the ideal number of members in a group be between five and eight, because they say that too many members make it too easy for some quiet members to remain passive and not actively participate to achieve the group's goals. They suggest that smaller groups allow for greater flexibility, especially for adjusting time schedules, and allow for increased participation and more control over group cohesion. Even though large groups can draw on more information from more members, this increased membership allows less time for individuals to participate. One possible compromise is that the larger group can break up into subgroups for certain tasks, with the smaller group meeting more frequently.

Group organization

Groups can be structured in a variety of ways, depending on their goals and the kinds of tasks they want to accomplish. For some support groups, an important question is whether or not there will be a group leader. In our experience, an effective facilitator is often crucial in facilitating the smooth functioning of a group. Among his or her responsibilities are starting the meeting, negotiating the agenda, focusing the discussion, and summarizing conclusions.

Determining group goals

Once the group has been formed, the issue of the group's goals must be addressed. Although a general goal for the group may have been decided prior to its formation, once the group has been formed, this goal can be renegotiated and refined by the whole group during the first few meetings. Wolff and Vera (1989) suggest that if the group members do not know each other, they may want to work toward short-term goals that can be achieved within a limited time frame. The teachers can later reevaluate the group's progress and formulate new or longer-term objectives.

Group time

Decisions about how much time to devote to a teacher support group will depend on the focus of the group and the commitments of its members.

Often it may be necessary to adjust the time arrangements, depending on what is happening elsewhere in the school.

Group meeting place

An appropriate meeting site is important if a group is to function effectively. Factors such as privacy, comfort, size, and distractions need to be taken into account.

Troubleshooting

As with any activity involving people with different perceptions, personalities, concerns, and goals, support groups can encounter problems. These can normally be resolved relatively easily as long as group members are committed to the success of the group and are willing listeners. Oliphant (2003) offers a number of suggestions that can help avoid problems. For example:

- Don't spend too much time on complaints, particularly those of one person. Focus on "achievements and accomplishments" as well.
- Offer feedback that is supportive.
- Remember that the purpose of the group is not to provide therapy for personal problems for which professional assistance might be advisable.
- Talk in meeting should be formal discussion, not informal teachers' lounge chat.
- Focus on the practical: Try new ideas instead of just talking about them.
- Focus on offering support and encouragement to each other in solving problems, rather than on complaining.

Summary

Teacher support groups offer a forum where teachers can discuss issues that are important to them, while at the same time getting support, advice, and help from other like-minded teachers in a nonthreatening environment. Many different types of groups are possible, depending on the goals and membership of the group. Support groups can help develop a culture of collaboration in an institution and enable teachers with different levels of training and experience to learn from one another and work together to explore issues and resolve problems.

Examples of teacher study groups

I. Teacher support group: EFL

A language teacher support group (for a full discussion, see Farrell, 1999) was formed in Seoul, South Korea. The following is an outline of what happened.

REASONS FOR FORMING THE GROUP

All of the four group members were (separately) on the lookout for a group in which they could find answers to various questions they had about teaching English language in Korea. Each member volunteered to come together as a group to talk about their work. However, one of the teachers was somewhat hesitant about the whole process of reflection. She said:

At first, I hesitated to join the group because of my tight schedule. But then I felt the need to take part, talk about our classes, and find out what was happening in them. I couldn't resist pushing myself into it.

GROUP MEMBERS

Group members consisted of a group facilitator, Tom, who initiated the group, and three other language teachers. Gender was split (two females and two males), as was ethnic background (two Asians and two Caucasians). The two female Asian teachers had 5 years of teaching experience, while the two Caucasian teachers had more than 10 years experience in teaching EFL. Two of the participants were teaching full-time at a university in Seoul, another was teaching part-time at a university in Seoul, and the other was teaching an English class at a private company in Seoul.

GROUP GOALS

The teacher support group came together in order to become more confident and reflective teachers. Initial goals were general in nature: to reflect on teaching, to discuss theory, and to observe each other teach.

GROUP ACTIVITIES

The teacher support group planned three different types of activities: group discussions, classroom observations, and writing journals about teaching. The four participants met together as a group once a week for 12 weeks to discuss their teaching. Each group meeting lasted for 3 hours. Tom led the discussions for the first few meetings about issues that he and other members considered important from classes they had taught during the previous week(s). However, as the group began to develop, the group members took turns leading the discussions about many diverse topics. The subjects the group talked about included life experiences, inability to deal with large classes, students' responses to questions in class, handling uninvolved students, material for conversation classes, giving feedback and the concept of what it is to be a teacher, encouraging students to work in groups, giving clear instructions, keeping questions open-ended, and writing directions on the chalkboard.

PROBLEMS

Although all group members said that they found the group meetings very supportive, some problems were encountered along the way. One problem concerned the lack of clearly defined goals for each meeting. Because the goals of each meeting were not specifically spelled out from the very beginning, some of the participants felt they had been unsure of the direction of the whole reflective process. This coincided with the different phases the group seemed to go through: the first phase, the "getting to know you phase," which lasted for about five meetings, and "the reflective phase," which continued for the remaining seven meetings. During the first phase, group members found it difficult to say anything about their teaching because they were still trying to establish trust: trust about what to reveal in public to other group members and trust about what the members might do with this knowledge. Additionally, even though all four agreed to write journals and observe each other teaching at the beginning of the reflective process, individual members interpreted these activities differently. For example, the group decided not to observe each other's classes and asked Tom, the facilitator, to observe and tape the classes alone. Eventually, one teacher decided to stop having her class observed for unexplained reasons. This same teacher also stopped writing her journal. The teacher said she that she was not comfortable being observed while teaching and that she did not want to write about teaching.

EVALUATING THE SUPPORT GROUP

Even though the group experienced some problems, all members found the experience worthwhile. They believe the group empowered them and made them better, if not more insightful, teachers and that other people working in such groups can receive the same benefits. For example, one member really enjoyed the group discussions:

The group members were great. I was especially fascinated by their attitude toward and enthusiasm about teaching. They didn't mind revealing how they think, prepare, and teach, and they accepted the differences between themselves and myself.

Another group member found that the group experience was a high point in his ESL teaching career. This was his first time he had experienced such reflections on his teaching:

I had never had the chance to talk about [teaching]... these conversations [which were about what had happened in the class but not exclusively so] became extremely important and exciting for me.

II. Teacher support group: ESL

This group (which members referred to as a learning circle) of ten primary school teachers from the same school came together with a language consultant and a facilitator from Teachers' Network Singapore (a government-funded network of teachers within the Ministry of Education, Singapore; for a full discussion, see Tang, 2001) in order to explore strategies for teaching grammar to the primary school students. Most of the students in the school come from a non-English-speaking home environment and are average or below average in language proficiency. They have problems speaking English with their peers in school and they hardly ever read books in English. This lack of oral and reading skills in English could have contributed to their weakness in written English. Also, they only had a basic understanding of grammar, and most teachers expressed concern about keeping the students' interest and attention during grammar classes. Therefore, ten teachers came together to discuss their main concern: how to make grammar classes not only interesting but also effective. It was hoped that through these sharing sessions, the teachers could adopt successful strategies.

GROUP GOALS

The members of the learning circle decided to try to answer the following questions:

1. What strategies can be used to motivate pupils to learn grammar effectively?

2. Is there a place for grammar drills and practice in the text-based approach to teaching grammar?

GROUP ACTIVITIES

Four different approaches to teaching grammar were introduced to the learning circle members over 3 months and the teachers tried them out in their respective classes: *focus on form, consciousness-raising, processing grammar instruction*, and *corrective feedback*. These were explained to the members in the following way.

Focus on form. Teachers teach grammar when the need arises during a meaning-focused activity. The example used to explain this approach was as follows: While engaged in a task of writing newspaper reports, a meaning-focused task, a student may encounter problems in understanding why and how the passive form is used in the English language. The teacher stops the students from carrying on with the task in order to focus their attention on the passive form.

Consciousness-raising. Teachers teach students grammar by raising the awareness of students to a particular grammatical item so that students can take note of the target structure. After highlighting the target grammar structure, students must compare the input given with their own speech or writing so that they can notice their errors ("noticing the gap"). Students are also made aware of the possibility of "noticing the hole," which means that even if they know the rule, they may be unable to reproduce the structure spontaneously in communicative situations.

Processing grammar instruction. Students are made aware of the meaning behind a grammar item. For example, to enable students to distinguish between the simple past and the past continuous tense, students can be given these two sentences to compare: *She was waiting at the bus stop; She waited at the bus stop.*

Corrective feedback. Teachers correct the students when they make errors either explicitly or implicitly.

The members practiced two or three approaches at each learning circle meeting. They also discussed how they could use these approaches in their classrooms, especially in an effective and fun way. The members of the learning circle decided to integrate the strategies with activities such as role-play, charades, and games.

EVALUATION OF THE GROUP

In order to evaluate the success of teaching grammar in this way, the teachers focused on past tenses in the students' compositions. Teachers found that the *consciousness-raising* approach was used most frequently by the learning circle members because it required minimal effort from the students and did not take much time away from the curriculum. Basically, the teachers told the students to underline all the past-tense words as they read a passage in their textbooks. Students were then asked to explain the function of the underlined words to see if they knew the rule. The students were then shown how the past tense can be used in their own narrative writing. The teachers then used the "notice the gap" strategy when getting students to examine if they used the past tense correctly in their own narrative writing. This was followed up with short written exercises that required the students to use the past tense spontaneously. After 6 weeks of this type of instruction, the students were given another piece of writing and the teachers found that the students used the past-tense verb forms more correctly.

The teachers also used strategies such as taking sentences from the students' compositions and putting them on transparencies for examination by the whole class. The teachers did use the *processing grammar instruction* and *focus on form* approaches but less frequently than the consciousness-raising approach.

The teachers in the learning circle concluded the following about their experiences reflecting on the teaching of grammar during the group project:

- Good teaching and learning of grammar must involve students as active learners.
- There must be a variety of learning activities in order to keep student interest.
- Bring the students' real-life experiences into the activities whenever possible.
- Grammar learning takes time in order for grammar to be internalized.
- It is better to expose students to environments where grammar is used correctly.
- Implementing an extensive reading program may help with indirect grammar learning.
- Grammar mistakes are inevitable and teachers may need to revisit the grammar structures students had been taught (in the form of drills).
- Grammar activities designed in the form of text types made grammar exercises less boring for the students.

Overall, the members of the learning circle found the sharing of ideas very useful as they picked up skills "to approach language teaching in a holistic fashion in line with current trends" (Ang et al., 2000, p. 71).

References and further reading

Belbin, R. M. (1993). *Team roles at work*. Oxford: Butterfield-Heinemann.

Bertcher, H. J., & Maple, F. (1996). *Creating groups*. Beverly Hills, CA: Sage.

Birchak, B., Connor, C., Crawford, K. M., Kahn, L. H., Kaser, S., Turner, S., & Short, K. (1998). *Teacher study groups*. Urbana, IL: National Council of Teachers of English.

Farrell, T. S. C. (1999). Reflective practice in a teacher development group. *System* 27(2), pp. 157–172.

Francis, D. (1995). The reflective journal: A window to preservice teachers' knowledge. *Teaching and Teacher Education,* 25(2), pp. 229–241.

James, P. (1996). Learning to reflect: A story of empowerment. *Teaching and Teacher Education* 12, pp. 81–97.

Kirk, W., & Walter, G. (1981). Teacher support groups serve to minimize teacher burnout: Principles for organizing. *Education* 102, pp. 147–150.

Lieberman, A., & Grolnick, M. (1998). Educational reform networks: Changes in the forms of reform. In A. Hargreaves, A. Liberman, M. Fullan, & D. Hopkins (Eds.), *International handbook of educational change* (pp. 710–729). Boston: Kluwer Academic.

Liou, H. C. (2001). Reflective practice in a preservice teacher education program for high school English teachers in Taiwan, ROC. *System* 29, pp. 197–208.

Matlin, M., & Short, K. G. (1991). How our teacher study group sparks change. *Educational Leadership* 49, p. 68.

Oliphant, K. (2003). Teacher development groups: Growth through cooperation (Appendix A). In G. Crooks, *A practicum in TESOL* (pp. 203–213). New York: Cambridge University Press.

Schultz, B. G. (1989). *Communicating in a small group: Theory and practice*. New York: HarperCollins.

Sitamparam, S., & Dhamotharan, M. (1992). Peer networking: Towards self-direction in teacher development. *English Teaching Forum* 30, pp. 12–15.

Tang, N. (2001). *A compilation of teacher research: Papers presented at the Learning Circle Carnival 2000*. Singapore: Teachers' Network.

Teachers' Network, Singapore. (2001). *Strategies for teaching grammar,*
  pp. 64–74.
Toseland, R., & Siporin, M. (1986). When to recommend group treatment:
  A review of the clinical and research literature. *International Journal
  of Group Psychotherapy* 36(2), pp. 171–201.
Wolff, L. B., & Vera, J. L. (1989). Teachers' groups in Spain. *Teacher
  Trainer* 3, pp. 14–16.

Appendix

Examples of teacher support group Web sites

MICROSOFT CLASSROOM TEACHER NETWORK

This Web site provides useful tips for teachers as well as viewpoints on
education. It also features best practices in teaching and in-depth interviews
with noted authorities on curriculum topics.
http://www.microsoft.com/education/?ID=mctn

LANGUAGE TEACHERS NETWORK

Teachers and educators share tips and resources. Includes free newsletter
and job bank for members.
http://www.languageteachingnetwork.com

5 *Keeping a teaching journal*

The nature of a teaching journal

A teaching journal is an ongoing written account of observations, reflections, and other thoughts about teaching, usually in the form of a notebook, book, or electronic mode, which serves as a source of discussion, reflection, or evaluation. The journal may be used as a record of incidents, problems, and insights that occurred during lessons; it may be an account of a class that the teacher would like to review or return to later; or it may be a source of information that can be shared with others. The following account by a language teacher describes what she learned from keeping a teaching journal.

Vignette

Recently, I realized from keeping a journal that I tended to focus more on what the class was supposed to be doing, that is, on the lesson plan and the content, and not as much as I should on what the students were actually doing with the material. Moreover, the teaching journal disciplined me to analyze the same students doing basically the same thing day after day until I got this insight from looking at various entries over time in my journal. In other words, I saw this pattern in my classes and I realized that just because I taught the lesson did not mean that the students learned that preplanned lesson. Now I try to answer four questions every day as I write in my journal: What did my students learn today? What helped them learn? What got in the way? What specific evidence can I quote to back up my claims? Because I know that I have a record of my lessons that I can access easily, I can't wait to get back into the classroom the next day to find out what my students are going to do next and see if my reflections are correct. Now I begin to experience the lesson as my students experience it. I am in their shoes!

Jane Hoelker

Reflection

- Why did journal writing help Jane discover things about her teaching?
- What benefits can you see in keeping a teaching journal?

Purpose and benefits of a teaching journal

Journal writing enables a teacher to keep a record of classroom events and observations. We have found that without such a record, the teacher often has no substantial recollection of what happened during a lesson and cannot use the experience of successful (and sometimes unsuccessful) teaching as a source for further learning. The process of writing about teaching events often leads to new insights about those events.

Vignette

Managing time and activities during a lesson is a separate skill from pre-lesson planning. As a professional development project, a colleague and I teaching a parallel language class decided to monitor our interactive decision making during a one-semester course. We decided to explore these questions:

1. When and why did we depart from our teaching plans?
2. What can we learn from each other's changes?

We both kept a teaching journal and after each lesson we noted changes in our own prewritten plan. Then, midway through the course and again at the end, we used our account of the changes we made as the basis for comparing our approach to teaching and to the course. We found that the main reasons that prompted us to depart from our lesson plans were timing reasons, affective reasons, including group dynamics and the class "atmosphere," to bring about variety in teaching style, to promote learner involvement, to adjust the difficulty level, as a response to problems with the course book task, or for organizational reasons. Some changes resulted from multiple reasons. In our discussion we noted that one of us made more changes than the other and we discussed whether making fewer changes was the sign of a better planner or whether in fact the "fewer changes" person had made other changes but had not recorded them. On the whole, we found the experience extremely useful and discovered a number of things about our teaching that we had not been fully aware of.

Marilyn Lewis

Reflection

- What are some advantages of sharing a journal with other teachers? What might be some disadvantages?
- How much time do you think the procedures described in this vignette would take?

Journal writing can help a teacher question, explore, and analyze how he or she teaches and can also provide a basis for conversations with peers or a supervisor. Journal writing can serve different purposes, depending on who the audience for a journal is. For teachers, a journal can serve as a way of clarifying their own thinking and of exploring their own beliefs and practices. It can be used to monitor their own practices, to provide a record of their teaching for others to read, and to document successful teaching experiences. And it can provide a way of collaborating with other teachers in exploring teaching issues. For peers, supervisors, and mentors, reading and responding to a teacher's journal can serve as means of encouraging reflective inquiry and can facilitate resolving problems and concerns.

Writing a teaching journal provides an "opportunity for teachers to use the process of writing to describe and explore their own teaching practices" (Ho & Richards, 1993, p. 8). Through different forms of journal writing – individual writing, writing for a peer, group or dialogue journal writing – a teacher can step back from an experience for a moment in order to create an understanding of what the experience means. However, as we and others have found, writing a teaching journal is not without its difficulties. These difficulties include whether to share the journal with another reader, the difficulty for some people of writing reflectively, and the time demands of journal writing. Nevertheless, journal writing offers a simple way of becoming more aware of one's teaching and learning. By writing down one's observations, thoughts, and stories over time, one can see patterns emerge, and when interpretations of these patterns are made, one often also sees growth and development. Within the context of language teaching, writing a journal allows the telling and retelling of experiences so that others may also benefit from them. Ho and Richards (1993), in a survey of thirty-two teachers who had kept journals, found that 71 percent of the teachers found it useful, 25 percent found it fairly useful, and only 4 percent did not enjoy writing a journal. Here are some things language teachers said about journal writing:

- Writing a journal forces you to reflect on certain issues and bring them out into the open.
- Journal writing gets you thinking about things that are unconsciously going on in the mind.

- It enables you to discover the importance of relating your own experience of learning to that of the pupils you teach.
- It enhances awareness about the way you teach and how students learn.
- It serves as a means of generating questions and hypotheses about teaching and the learning process.
- It is the most natural form of classroom research.
- It promotes the development of reflective teaching.

Procedures used for keeping a journal

Journal writing can be in the form of computer word processing (individual), electronic mail (group), and even through "talk" – by speaking journal entries into a recorder for later analysis. All or parts of the tape can be transcribed, if needed. An advantage of electronic journals is that they can be sent to peers, supervisors, and/or teacher-educators easily and for immediate feedback and comment. Additionally, two teachers can collaborate on the actual writing of the entries to make them truly interactive journals. It is probably advisable to make hard copies of word-processed and electronic mail journals in order to keep records. The following vignette describes how a teacher in Turkey uses an electronic journal (e-journal) to facilitate her professional development.

Vignette
E-learning journals have become an integral part of my personal and professional development in my teaching career. As a teacher, I have been critically reflecting upon my teaching process for 2 years now through an e-learning journal. The reflective writing itself through the weekly e-learning journal entries I make has focused my thinking on the issues concerning my course design, its implementation, and its evaluation. Moreover, because of systematically writing in my e-journal, I have been more encouraged to maintain a structured level of planning, monitoring, and evaluation of these issues by my reflections on these entries. This systematic and ongoing interaction through the e-learning journal has made me become a more critically thinking teacher. Furthermore, I have developed a more positive attitude in using IT in my personal and professional development as well as in my classroom teaching.

Ayse Yumuk

Reflection

- What are some advantages of keeping an electronic journal?
- What might be an advantage of keeping journal entries over a long period of time and looking back over them from time to time?

The following general procedures are recommended for keeping a written teaching journal (Richards & Lockhart, 1994; Ho & Richards, 1993):

1. Decide on your audience: yourself, a peer, and/or an instructor.
2. Decide on your focus: a lesson, a technique/method, a theory, a question posed.
3. Make entries on a regular basis (after a lesson, daily, or once a week).
4. Review what you have written regularly – every 2 or 3 weeks.

The audience for a teaching journal

There may be several audiences for a teaching journal. These include the writer, other teachers, and a supervisor.

The teacher

Often, the primary audience is the teacher. The journal serves as a personal record of thoughts, feelings, and reactions to teaching. Entries can be reread from time to time in order to learn from what was written. This is sometimes called an *intrapersonal journal* (Gebhard, 1999). An intrapersonal journal is a place where a teacher writes for himself or herself about day-to-day teaching concerns. This type of journal can also provide items to use in a teaching portfolio. An intrapersonal journal can also be useful when self-monitoring lessons (see Chapter 3). Entries can be reviewed for patterns that may have emerged over a period of time.

Other teachers

A journal may also be shared with other teachers and used as a basis for comparison, discussion, and further reflection. This is sometimes called a *dialogical journal*. This type of collaboration offers opportunities for teachers to support, and at times challenge, each other while exploring teaching. Colleagues can share what has worked or not worked in different classes and can also suggest solutions to problems or alternative methods of teaching. A dialogical journal can be especially helpful in a peer-coaching situation (see Chapter 10) in which two colleagues work together to reflect on their current practices, develop new skills in teaching, curriculum development, and/or materials development, or just to share ideas about the peer-coaching process itself. A teaching journal can also be useful for individual members in a teacher support group (see Chapter 4) and serve as a means of recording what members of the group feel would be a useful focus for their discussions. In the group, the members share their journals with one another, either simply for reading or for spoken or written comments by members of the group.

A supervisor

Sometimes a journal may be shared with a supervisor, who may find it a much richer source of information about a person's teaching than could be obtained from a brief classroom visit. When writing for a supervisor, the journal can sometimes be used to ask questions or ask for clarification. The supervisor or instructor can respond to journal entries through discussion or through written entries. When writing for a supervisor, the teacher might focus on aspects of teaching that provide evidence of ongoing professional development.

Responding to another teacher's journal

When a journal is shared with another teacher or a supervisor, the reader will normally write responses to entries, comment on observations, offer suggestions, or perhaps answer questions. Responses can be of several different kinds.

- *Affective and personalizing comments.* These comments are intended to establish rapport with the person writing the journal and to reduce feelings of anxiety. These usually include comments that are encouraging, such as "Great idea!" or "What an interesting question!"
- *Procedural comments.* These comments might consist of suggestions based on problems or questions the writer has posed. These comments might also include expectations of the teacher-educator or peer teacher. Examples of such a comment would be "I think we may need to meet more regularly to exchange journals," "Where do you want me to write my comments?" and "Are you going to focus your journal writing on the advanced listening class?"
- *Direct responses to questions.* Sometimes teachers may want a direct reply to the questions they pose because they require knowledge in order

to solve a particular problem or dilemma. Examples of such responses include: "I like that you focused on a top-down approach to the teaching of reading for this class. However, you wondered how exactly you could adapt prediction for your class. I usually show the class the title of the passage and ask them to guess what the story will be about. Then I sometimes use a DRTA (directed-reading thinking activity) to chunk the text in each paragraph and have the students continue using the prediction strategy. We can meet if you want to discuss this."

- *Understanding responses.* Because language teaching is a complex activity full of uncertainties for new teachers, understanding responses from peers can alleviate some of the teacher's anxieties. An example of this type of response would mirror the author's feelings or ideas, such as: "You know I fully understand your reluctance to force your shy students to speak in your conversation class; however, I would remind them that one of the only means of improving their conversation skills is to practice in and during class. I also wonder how much of the 'shyness' is language anxiety and how much is culture-based. What do you think?"

- *Exploratory suggestions.* These suggestions can help the teacher explore in more depth and thus gain a greater awareness of his or her teaching. For example: "I also agree that teaching writing involves having our students write multiple drafts of their texts. Next is what issues within writing they should focus on during each rewrite. Is it grammar? or organization? or what? I have my students focus on organization *after* they have written their first drafts and on grammar only after their next-to-final draft. Do you think you might want to try this method?"

- *Synthesis comments and questions.* These comments are important comments because links that may not have been clear earlier (in previous journal entries) become more obvious. Synthesis-type comments help the teacher clarify earlier journal questions, such as: "In your first few journal entries you mentioned that you had wanted your students to talk more to each other (in English) in class. Recently, you wrote that your students are now talking to each other (in English) more than you are lecturing. What do you think caused this turnaround? Do you think it could be related to our journal 'discussions' on seating arrangements? Or do you think it could be related to the change in seating arrangements you made (from rows to a big circle)?"

- *Unsolicited comments and questions.* These questions can help focus on an issue (or issues) that the teacher may have forgotten or avoided. Sometimes it is easier for an objective reader to read between the lines, thus providing the journal author with an alternative point of view. These comments can be in the form of a question or comment such as: "I see that you have written twenty entries in your teaching journal in the past 12 weeks, which is really great. However, one pattern that I notice is your reluctance to look at the communication patterns in your conversation classes, yet you wonder if you are talking too much. Also, in one journal entry you said that your students did not answer your questions fast enough. What do you think would be reasons for your students' reluctance to answer questions? I would also be interested to know what you think of the communication patterns in your class."

Program coordinators may want to encourage their teachers to make regular journal entries in the stream-of-consciousness mode outlined in this chapter. These can be edited later and included in the teachers' teaching portfolios as evidence of their reflections. Of course, teachers may be encouraged to form groups and reflect on their journal entries together (see the example near the end of this chapter of three teachers who came together to reflect on their journal entries [Brock, Yu, & Wong, 1992]).

Implementing journal writing

In our experience, in order to carry out journal writing successfully, a number of factors need to be kept in mind.

1. *Set goals for journal writing.* Decide why you want to do journal writing and what you hope to get out of it. If you do not have any specific focus, and you only want to write about your practice in general terms, then try to suspend judgment and select any general theme (e.g., "A class I will never forget") and write for a fixed period of time.
2. *Decide who your audience is.* Will you be writing for yourself, for peers, or for a supervisor? How will this influence what you write about and how you write about it?
3. *Be prepared to set aside time for journal writing.* Journal writing takes time, and teachers who wish to make use of it will need to set aside up to 2 or more hours per week for this activity. A decision has to be made concerning how many entries to make and what length entries will be. Answers to both questions will depend on the purpose of writing the journal.
4. *Set a time frame for the writing activity.* It's not necessary to spend time planning and revising a journal entry. It is better simply to write without stopping for about 6 to 10 minutes without worrying about spelling, grammar, or organization. However, if your entries are to be

read by a supervisor, you might wish to review them later for content and organization.

5. *Review your journal entries regularly to see what you can learn from them.* It is important to review your entries from time to time and to try to make connections between entries or to see what ideas and understanding emerge.

6. *Evaluate your journal writing experience to see if it meets your goals.* Reread your journal after a time to see if it achieved what you had intended, whether it was in order to document successful experiences, to gain new awareness, or to share experiences with a colleague.

Richards and Lockhart (1994, pp. 16–17) suggest various questions that can be used as an initial guide when starting a teaching journal. One or more of the questions could be the focus of a journal entry.

I. Questions about your teaching
1. What did you set out to teach?
2. Were you able to accomplish these goals?
3. What teaching materials did you use? How effective were they?
4. What techniques did you use?
5. What grouping arrangements did you use?
6. Was your lesson teacher-dominated?
7. What kind of teacher-student interaction occurred?
8. Did anything amusing or unusual occur?
9. Did you have any problems with the lesson?
10. Did you do anything differently than usual?
11. What kinds of decision making did you employ?
12. Did you depart from your lesson plan? If so, why? Did the change make things better or worse?
13. What was the main accomplishment of the lesson?
14. Which parts of the lesson were most successful?
15. Which parts of the lesson were least successful?
16. Would you teach the lesson differently if you taught it again?
17. Was your philosophy of teaching reflected in the lesson?
18. Did you discover anything new about your teaching?
19. What changes do you think you should make in your teaching?

II. Questions about the students
1. Did you interact with all of the students in the class today?
2. Did students contribute actively to the lesson?
3. How did you respond to different students' needs?
4. Were students challenged by the lesson?

5. What do you think students really learned from the lesson?
6. What did they like most about the lesson?
7. What didn't they respond well to?

III. Questions about yourself as a language teacher
1. What is the source of my ideas about language teaching?
2. Where am I in my professional development?
3. How am I developing as a language teacher?
4. What are my strengths as a language teacher?
5. What are my limitations at present?
6. Are there any contradictions in my teaching?
7. How can I improve my language teaching?
8. How am I helping my students?
9. What satisfaction does language teaching give me?

The following vignette shows how a teacher in a Japanese university uses journal writing to help her improve aspects of her teaching.

Vignette

"Need to keep it stimulating for those guys who have lots of ideas." Students had done a survey outside class on meat eating and vegetarianism. The task of the class was to write a report on what they had found out, in a group of four, and then feed back their report to the whole class. While watching students perform this task I became more strongly aware of the difference in levels within the class. When it came to listening to the feedback, the more able students were clearly bored listening to their more hesitant classmates.

Ellen Head

Reflection

- What advice would you give Ellen to deal with the problem she describes?
- What other kinds of problems sometimes arise in mixed-level classes?

Writing thoughts and observations

There are two approaches to writing down one's thoughts and observations in a journal.

- *Stream-of-consciousness approach.* When writing for oneself, a "stream-of-consciousness" type of writing may be all that is necessary, where grammar, style, or organization is less important than obtaining a record of teaching and feelings and thoughts about it. This exploratory type of writing can generate lots of ideas and awareness that can be looked at after some time and analyzed for recurring patterns.

• *Edited approach.* When writing for another teacher or for a supervisor, a more edited writing style may be helpful. Written entries by the peer or instructor can be made in the margins of the journal.

The following shows how a teacher in Thailand organizes his teaching journal.

Vignette

To avoid having to keep a journal for too long (and to gain the most benefit), I try to find a specific point about my work that I would like to know more about. Although these points are frequently about my classroom teaching, this need not be the case. For example, recently I was involved in the design of a new English support course for IT students at the university where I work. Although I had fairly extensive experience in course design, it struck me that in my previous attempts at designing courses I had often arrived at a finished product without really knowing where it came from. Given the importance of course design for student learning, this was clearly an unsatisfactory state of affairs, so I decided to keep a journal throughout the process of designing the English for IT course to see how I actually reached key decisions affecting the nature of the course. To this end, after meetings with staff from the IT faculty, after meetings with language department colleagues, and after those occasions when I sat down by myself to work on the new course, I tried to spend 15 minutes or so jotting down thoughts and reflections on the course design process. In doing this, I tried to engage in a stream-of-consciousness process to the extent that my speed of writing allowed. After a few weeks, I had a rather disorganized pile of paper full of my thoughts on course design. This was all well and good and it would have been easy to stop there. However, to gain a real understanding of the process of course design, I needed to do something with the journals once I had finished writing them. The first thing I did was to read through them like a teacher writing down questions and comments asking for more clarification, explanation, and especially reasons. I then went through the journals again, adding points to try and answer my own questions in retrospect. After that, in effect, I analyzed my journals as a research study looking for patterns and focusing on frequently mentioned and salient points. I then compared what I had done with the literature on course design. From all of this, I learned that the process I was following was a bit of a hotchpotch of stages with sudden jumps as I made some decisions based largely on my own preferences. I also became worried about how decisions were made before any needs analysis had been conducted. This gave me plenty to ponder and evaluate, and the next time I was involved in course design I made efforts to ensure that key decisions derived from needs rather than my own biases.

Richard Watson Todd

Reflection

- What are some advantages of writing a stream-of-consciousness-type journal?
- Why do you think Richard edits his own writing?

Posner (1996) suggests the following general format for dialogue journals:

- *Date and time of entry.* A journal entry should only cover one day and should be written on the day of the event; otherwise, we may forget exactly what happened and when.
- *Brief sequencing of the events.* Make a brief list describing what happened (all the events). This helps you keep a record of what happened.
- *Elaboration of details of an event.* Select one or two events that are significant to you – that excited you, bothered you, or made you think again about an issue. Next, describe the events in detail, how you felt about them at the time, and how your students responded to them.
- *Analysis of the event.* Suggest an explanation for the event, saying why it was significant to you and how you interpret it.

The following is an example of an edited teaching journal from an EFL grammar class in Korea. The vignette outlines the sequence of events that happened at the beginning of the class.

Vignette

Sequence of events of class beginning
- Started class as usual
- Went over homework
- Noticed that most students did not do the homework
- Was annoyed and frustrated

Events

We (the class and myself) went over the grammar exercises (articles *a*, *an*, and *the*) that I had given for homework (because they always make many mistakes in articles in their writing) for the first 15 minutes. I had tried to make these grammar exercises interesting for the students by proving handouts that challenged their knowledge to (*a*) recognize that there was a grammar mistake and (*b*) try to give the correct answer. I have found that my students are so used to doing the fill-in-the-blank-type grammar exercises that they do not have to think about why there may be a mistake. So, my main reason for providing a passage with all the English articles omitted was to get the students thinking about their knowledge of grammar (recognizing that there is a mistake in the first place) and then correcting that mistake. I hope they will use this system in their peer-editing of compositions too.

Episode

After about 10 minutes in which I was going around the class asking the students for their answers, I noticed that many of them had not done their homework. I was very disappointed because I had spent a long time preparing this homework sheet (handout) and I had thought long and hard about how I wanted to teach articles to these students because of the quantity of mistakes in their written and oral work. I felt really annoyed that these students did not appreciate the work I was doing for them or the fact that they were not motivated enough to correct their misuse of articles in their writing and speaking. This never really happened in any of my classes before.

Analysis

At this stage I can't really say that I came up with any clear solution to the problem. Was it that they were just not motivated to study grammar or articles in particular? Was this the reason they all did not complete their homework assignment? Or was it because they did not know how to complete the assignment? Maybe they are not used to this sort of grammar assignment (first find the mistake and then correct it). Maybe it is because they were used to fill-in-the-blank-style exercises? I think I should have explained this type of grammar exercise in more detail and shown them why it is very useful for their grammar development. I still wonder what the underlying cause is for their resistance.

Eric Harmsen

Reflection

- Who do you think is the primary audience for Eric's journal entry?
- What do you think Eric learned from writing about this event?

Choosing topics to write about

We would emphasize that journal writing should have a purpose and not be an activity in which the teacher engages simply for the sake of it. Productive topics might include the teacher's personal learning, development, and growth, or thoughts about problems that occur inside and outside the classroom. Sometimes the focus may be a specific issue the teacher would like to explore through journal writing, and most of his or her entries will be related to this issue. Such issues could include the following:

- Evaluations of lessons taught, that is, focusing on what worked well, what didn't work so well, something the teacher might do differently next time
- Changes made to a lesson plan
- How errors of grammar or pronunciation were dealt with
- Vocabulary problems that occurred during a lesson
- Problems encountered and how the teacher responded to them
- Problems the teacher feels he or she has to overcome and suggestions as to how to go about addressing them
- Monitoring of some problem learners in terms of slow progress in speaking, listening, and/or writing
- Ideas that occurred concerning how to make better use of a reading text
- How the teacher dealt with classroom management problems
- How the teacher deals with students who continuously speak in their native language during class
- How to deal with different cultural groups within one class

---

Vignette

Recently, a colleague suggested that I focus [in my teaching journal] on success, writing about the things that went well and trying to account for them. That was a delightful idea for me. Now I write about both "problem" lessons and successful ones. As I reread my notes from last term, I feel a growing sense of the sequence of class events as a process.

Ellen Head

Reflection

- What do you think a teacher can learn by writing about his or her successes in teaching?
- How do you think writing about a problem in teaching can sometimes suggest a solution to the problem?

Summary

Journal writing enables teachers to document teaching experiences and to use the process of writing about them as means of reflecting on teaching. Journal entries also provide information that can trigger useful conversations with peers and supervisors. Although journal-writing procedures are fairly straightforward, successful implementation of journal writing requires careful thought about its goals, its focus, and the time demands it can create for both writers and readers.

Example of a case study of journal writing

Getting started

A group of English language teachers in Hong Kong (Brock, Yu, & Wong, 1992) explored their teaching by writing journals throughout a 10-week term. They wanted to record and reflect on their teaching. Instead of keeping individual diaries, they decided to share them with each other regularly. Each teacher planned to keep diaries of two classes per week over a 10-week term. Entries were made for a range of different classes, and they did not narrow their focus to a few issues.

The process

Each week they read each other's journal and made written responses. They also met weekly (1-hour meetings) to talk about their entries, as well as to analyze and synthesize recurring issues and concerns. They wrote three diary entries each week, for 10 weeks, on different classes. They wrote in a "stream-of-consciousness" style, paying little attention to grammatical correctness or stylistic coherence. They exchanged journals and asked each other questions about their entries.

The outcome

At the end of the process, they all expressed conflicting emotions about what they had experienced. On the one hand, they found that writing a journal was valuable for them because of the insights they achieved from writing and reading each other's journals. On the other hand, they noted that the act of keeping a diary required discipline and regular journal writing became a burden on their time and energies. Additionally, the group realized that they should have focused on a few issues in depth rather than attempting to explore many issues at one time. Generally, though, they had positive reflections on the process as a whole as they discovered new suggestions and ideas from each other for approaching particular teaching tasks. It enabled them to gain new insights into other teachers' experiences.

Some insights

This case study of three English language teachers is a good example of the usefulness of writing a teaching journal and how teachers can benefit from sharing their journals with other teachers. However, in the future, teachers should make sure that they have enough time available to discipline themselves to write (and possibly share) their journals.

References and further reading

Bailey, K. M. (1983). Competitiveness and anxiety in adult second language learning: Looking at and through the diary studies. In H. W. Seliger & M. H. Long (Eds.), *Classroom-oriented research in second language acquisition* (pp. 67–102). Rowley, MA: Newbury House.

Bailey, K. M. (1990). The use of diary studies in teacher education programs. In J. C. Richards & D. Nunan (Eds.), *Second language teacher education* (pp. 215–226). New York: Cambridge University Press.

Boud, D. (2001). Using journal writing to enhance reflective practice. *New Directions for Adult and Continuing Education* 90, pp. 9–18.

Brinton, D. M., Holten, C. A., & Goodwin, J. M. (1993). Responding to dialogue journals in teacher preparation: What's effective? *TESOL Journal* 2(4), pp. 15–19.

Brock, M., Yu, B., & Wong, M. (1992). "Journalling" together: Collaborative diary-keeping and teacher development. In J. Flowerdew, M. Brock, & S. Hsia (Eds.), *Perspectives on second language teacher development* (pp. 295–307). Hong Kong: City University of Hong Kong.

Crandall, J. A. (2000). Language teacher education. *Annual Review of Applied Linguistics* 20, pp. 34–55.

Farrell, T. S. C. (1998). Teacher development through journal writing. *RELC Journal* 29(1), pp. 92–109.

Flowerdew, J., Brock, M., & Hsia, S. (Eds.). (1992). *Perspectives on second language teacher education*. Kowloon: City Polytechnic of Hong Kong.

Gebhard, J. G. (1999). Reflecting through a teaching journal. In J. G. Gebhard & R. Oprandy (Eds.), *Language teaching awareness* (pp. 78–98). Cambridge: Cambridge University Press.

Hiemstra, R. (2001). Uses and benefits of journal writing. *New Directions for Adult and Continuing Education* 90, pp. 19–26.

Ho, B., & Richards, J. C. (1993). Reflective thinking through teacher journal writing: Myths and realities. *Prospect: A Journal of Australian TESOL* 8, pp. 7–24.

Hoover, L. (1994). Reflective writing as a window on pre-service teachers' thought processes. *Teacher and Teacher Education* 10, pp. 83–93.

Jarvis, J. (1992). Using diaries for teacher reflection on in-service courses. *English Language Teaching Journal* 46(2), pp. 133–142.

McDonough, J. (1994). A teacher looks at teachers' diaries. *English Language Teaching Journal* 18, pp. 57–65.

Numrich, C. (1996). On becoming a language teacher: Insights from diary studies. *TESOL Quarterly* 30(1), pp. 131–153.

Orem, R. A. (2001). Journal writing in adult ESL: Improving practice through reflective writing. *New Directions for Adult and Continuing Education* 90, pp. 69–77.

Posner, G. J. (1996). Field Experience: A guide to reflective teaching (4th ed). White Plains, NY: Longman.

Richards, J. C. (1990). Beyond training: Approaches to teacher education in language teaching. *Language Teacher* 14, pp. 3–8.

Richards, J. C., & Lockhart, C. (1994). *Reflective teaching.* Cambridge: Cambridge University Press.

Richards, J. C., & Nunan, D. (Eds.) (1990). *Second language teacher education.* New York: Cambridge University Press.

Shin, S. J. (2003). The reflective L2 writing teacher. *English Language Teaching Journal* 57(1), pp. 3–11.

Woodfield H., & Lazarus, E. (1998). Diaries: A reflective tool on an INSET language course. *English Language Teaching Journal* 52(4), pp. 315–322.

6 *Peer observation*

The nature of peer observation

Peer observation refers to a teacher or other observer closely watching and monitoring a language lesson or part of a lesson in order to gain an understanding of some aspect of teaching, learning, or classroom interaction. In Chapter 3 we examined how teachers can observe their own classrooms. In this chapter the focus is on observing another teacher's classroom and what two teachers can gain through observing each other's teaching. In our experience, many teachers have a negative reaction to the idea of someone observing their classes. For many, "observation" calls to mind a coordinator or visitor coming to a classroom to carry out a supervisory or evaluative observation as part of the process of performance appraisal. Observation tends to be identified with evaluation, and consequently it is often regarded as a threatening or negative experience. Williams (1989, p. 86) has summed up some of the problems of traditional classroom observations:

- The teachers did not like it. It was threatening, frightening, and regarded as an ordeal.
- It was prescriptive.
- The checklist focused on too much at once.
- The teachers had no responsibility for the assessment. It was trainer-centered.

In this chapter we wish to separate evaluation from observation and explore how observation can be a part of the process of teacher development rather than focus on it as a component of appraisal.

Purpose and benefits of peer observation

Observation is a basic part of the learning of many occupations, particularly in vocational and technical fields, but learning through the observation of practitioners at work also plays a role in other fields, such as business, law, and medicine. In teaching, observation provides an opportunity for novice teachers to see what more experienced teachers do when they teach a lesson and how they do it. But experienced teachers can also benefit from peer observation. It provides an opportunity for the teacher to see how someone else deals with many of the same problems teachers face on a daily basis. A teacher might discover that a colleague has effective teaching strategies that the observer has never tried. Observing another teacher may also trigger reflections about one's own teaching. For the teacher being observed, the observer can provide an "objective" view of the lesson and can collect information about the lesson that the teacher who is teaching the lesson might not otherwise be able to gather. For both teachers, observation also has social benefits. It brings teachers together who might not normally have a chance to interact and provides an opportunity for the sharing of ideas and expertise, as well as a chance to discuss problems and concerns. Observation provides a chance to see how other teachers teach, it is a means of building collegiality in a school, it can be a way of collecting information about teaching and classroom processes, it provides an opportunity to get feedback on one's teaching, and it is a way of developing self-awareness of one's own teaching. The following vignette from a teacher in Korea illustrates how feedback from peer observation helped him develop as a teacher.

Vignette

I did not realize that I was asking and answering all my own questions until the observer showed me his narrative account of what he had seen in my class. I wanted to get on with the lesson and get them writing. Now I think my students just waited each time I asked questions because they realized that I would eventually answer these same questions for them. I was in fact spoon-feeding them too much. Now, thinking about this I realize that I frequently do this in my ESL classes. I think this is not helping my students. After this class and the discussion I had with the observer, I realized the power of having another pair of eyes in the room to help me "see" better. I should also say that the observer was a trusted friend and this helped me a lot too.

Eric Harmsen

Reflection

- Have you ever had an observer in your class? If so, what did you learn from the observer about your teaching?
- What are possible problems with having an observer in your class?

At the same time, the limitations of observation need to be understood. Obviously, an observer can only observe things that are visible. This includes such things as the following:

- *Timing*. How much time the teacher spends on different activities
- *Activities*. The types of activities the teacher employs during the lesson
- *Questioning techniques*. The types of questions the teachers asks
- *Participation*. Which learners actively participate in the lesson
- *Classroom language*. The kind of language learners produce

Other important aspects of the lesson, however, are not observable. They either have to be inferred or can only be identified as a result of talking to the teacher. These include the following:

- *Decision making*. The kinds of decisions the teacher considers during the lesson
- *Engagement*. The extent to which learners find aspects of the lesson interesting and engaging
- *Problems*. Difficulties the teacher experiences during the lesson but that might not have been visible to an observer
- *Teaching principles*. The principles that inform the teacher's approach to the lesson

Observation as a component of teacher development, therefore, involves discussion and reflection in order to arrive at a valid understanding of the meaning of the events observed.

Nonevaluative observation within the context of professional development is often welcomed by teachers, as the following teacher's comments reveal (from Richards, 1998).

- It revealed more detailed information on student performance during specific aspects of the lesson than I could have generated on my own.
- It revealed unexpected information about interaction between students during a lesson.
- It helped me develop a better working relationship with a colleague.

- It has taught me how much I can learn from my colleagues.
- It made me more aware of the limited range of teaching strategies that I have been using.
- I realized that I need to develop better time-management strategies.
- I have learned the value of evaluating myself. I know more about my strengths as a teacher as well.

If observation is to be a positive experience, however, it needs to be carefully planned for and implemented. The nature of observation might seem to be self-evident, yet the process of observation is more complex than it might appear. Lessons are dynamic and, to some extent, unpredictable events. They involve many different participants and often several different things are happening simultaneously. Classroom events sometimes unfold very quickly, so taking note of multiple events in real time is often impossible. Specific procedures are therefore needed.

Procedures used for peer observation

The purpose of observation is to learn from the observation experience. In order to do this, the observer cannot simply depend on memory. Procedures are needed that can be used to record information about the observation. We have made use of the following procedures, depending on the purpose of the observation.

Written narrative

This technique was described in Chapter 3 and involves a narrative account of the lesson as a whole. In the present context, however, the narrative is written by the observer rather than the teacher. The observer tries to provide an account of the main structure and development of the lesson, the kinds of activities the teacher employed, and the significant time periods within the lesson. In carrying out a written narrative, it is important not to try to describe everything that happens during the lesson. The language used should be objective and precise, and any form of evaluation should be avoided.

- *Advantages*. A written narrative provides a broad picture of a lesson and can be useful in helping to see what the structure of the lesson was like and how the teacher implemented or departed from his or her lesson plan.

- *Disadvantages*. Many aspects of the lesson are difficult to describe accurately in real time, such as the actual language that was used during a teacher–student exchange.

Field notes

Field notes consist of brief descriptions in note form of key events that occurred throughout the lesson, including interpretations of incidents where relevant. Taking notes is an informal way of jotting down observations of events as they occur. Notes are sometimes time-based (e.g., notes are made at regular intervals, such as every 5 minutes, using an observation form that identifies the time intervals that are being described), or they may be linked to the key activities that occurred during the lesson (e.g., the teacher's setting up and explanation of an activity, the teacher's comments on an activity after it has been completed).

- *Advantages*. Taking notes is a flexible way of observing a lesson. When significant things are happening, the observer notes down relevant information. When relatively little is happening (e.g., when students are silently reading a text), the observer can focus on something else (e.g., noting down how often students used their dictionary during a reading activity).
- *Disadvantages*. The information collected may be insufficient to capture what is really going on in the lesson.

Checklists

A checklist is a structured inventory listing features of a lesson that the observer completes as he or she observes the lesson (see Appendix for examples).

- *Advantages*. A checklist is highly focused and relatively easy to complete. It provides a systematic way of collecting information on specific aspects of a lesson.
- *Disadvantages*. Some aspects of a lesson are difficult to identify using a checklist. Checklists sometimes focus on trivial aspects of the lesson and fail to account for much of what happens.

In the following vignette, a teacher in Pakistan who wanted to observe the teaching practices used by the teachers while teaching reading and writing designed her own checklists. She discusses the process of designing her own checklists.

Vignette

For me, a classroom observation checklist must not contain too many items. This is a lesson I learned from a few observations I conducted. Sometime back, in order to appear very professional and show off my newly acquired knowledge, I developed wonderfully detailed checklists divided and sub-divided into many topics. The checklists looked very well done and highly useful, but in practice that was not the case. I ended up with too much to look for in too little time. So now, when I design checklists I restrict myself to looking at one or two aspects of my teaching and I do not devise too many questions, nor do I have too many categories. If you keep your checklist concise and stick to the most important points, your observation will be "good."

Aamna Khalid

Reflection

- What (and how many) items do you think are essential to include in a checklist for looking at a teacher's questioning behavior?
- What aspects of a lesson do you think can successfully be documented using a checklist?

The focus of an observation

Many aspects of a lesson can be the focus of an observation. Typical "how-to" dimensions of teaching include the following:

- How the teacher starts and ends a lesson
- How the teacher allots time within a lesson
- How the teacher assigns tasks to students
- How the teacher deals with a reticent student
- How the teacher organizes learning groups
- How the teacher supervises students while they are learning
- How the teacher asks questions

In focusing on the teacher's use of questions, observation can examine the following aspects of questions (from Gebhard, 1996).

- What kinds of questions does the teacher ask most often? Yes/no? Either/or?
- Wh-? Tag?

- What is the content of the teacher's questions?
- How long does the teacher wait after asking a question to get a response?
- How does the teacher give instructions? How much time does it take? Do students know what to do after being given the instructions?

Other topics that are suitable for classroom observations include the following:

- *Teacher's time management.* Allotment of time to different activities during the lesson
- *Students' performance of tasks.* Students' language use, procedures, and interaction patterns
- *Time on task.* The extent to which the students were actively engaged during a task
- *Teacher's action zone.* The extent to which the teacher interacted with some students more frequently than others during a lesson
- *Use of the textbook.* The extent to which a teacher used the textbook during a lesson and the types of departures made from it
- *Pair and group work.* The way students completed a task, the responses they made during the task, the type of language they used, students' time on task during pair and group work, and the dynamics of group activities

The following vignette is an example of how a recently qualified (nonnative English speaker) teacher of EFL, who was teaching English conversation classes in Korea for the first time, asked one of his peers (also a newly qualified native speaker of English) to observe him teach a series of lessons. However, he wanted her to focus specifically on interactions (teacher-to-student and student-to-student) in his classroom as he was unsure of what was happening. After the first two classroom observations, the observer noted that not all the students participated equally during group (student-to-student) work and that only certain students were involved when volunteering answers in whole-class discussions. After the discussions with the observer, the teacher came up with the following change, explained in his own words.

Vignette

Maybe I should ask students to form groups of four and ask them to tally their group's responses and ask each group to present their analysis. I will give each member a task such as group leader, group timekeeper, reporter, and secretary. I read this somewhere, and I think this could involve more participation from the students, rather than me doing the tallying, which became monotonous after a short while, and there wasn't any analysis of any kind of the results.

The teacher decided that he would like to learn from this discovery, so he asked the observer to observe him again to see if he was successful in implementing his new approach to group work. The beginning teacher commented on the outcome:

I saw a big difference in my classroom interactions when I asked them to form groups of four and gave each member a role in the group. They really got involved in the discussions as did the whole class. No one member of each group dominated the conversation and no one member was silent – all seemed happy with their assigned roles and duties. The peer-observation process really worked well for me, and I am happy I was able to ask another teacher whom I trust, because she is relatively new to teaching as well.

Park Sang Kang

Reflection

- Why do you think Sang Kang had difficulties realizing what type of interactions were common in his classes?
- How do you think peer observers can be helpful to beginning teachers? Experienced teachers?

When observation is a component of professional development, the focus may be on general teaching issues such as those noted here, or it could be directed toward concerns a teacher has about some aspect of his or her teaching. For example, it might be directed to issues such as the following:

- I have a feeling that the brighter students are not challenged by my teaching.
- I suspect that I spend too much time explaining things.
- Some students are too talkative, and some are too quiet, in my classes.

Observation by a peer could help the teacher further understand these problems by collecting information related to each problem.

Peer coaching

Peer coaching is a particular form of peer observation and involves an experienced teacher working with a less experienced teacher in a mentoring role. Peer coaching is the focus of Chapter 10.

Implementing peer observation

The following guidelines have proved useful for implementing peer observation:

- *Select a colleague to work with.* This may be a teacher who is teaching the same course or using the same textbook as you, or you could observe a teacher teaching a different kind of class, depending on mutual interest.
- *Each teacher takes turns at teaching and observing, as follows:*
  1. Arrange for a pre-observation orientation session. Before each observation, meet to discuss the nature of the class to be observed, the kind of material being taught, the teacher's approach to teaching, the kinds of students in the class, typical patterns of interaction and class participation, and any problems expected. The aim of these discussions is for the observer to understand the kinds of issues the teacher is facing and to learn more about the class and what its particular circumstances or problems are. The teacher who is teaching the lesson should also identify a focus for the observation at this stage and set a task for the observer to carry out. The observer's role is to collect information for the teacher that he or she would not normally be able to collect alone. It is important to stress that this task should not involve any form of evaluation.
  2. Decide on observation procedures to be used and arrange a schedule for the observations.
  3. Complete the observation using the procedures that were agreed on.
  4. Arrange a post-observation session. Meet as soon as possible after the lesson. The observer reports on the information collected and discusses it with the teacher.

Supporting teachers in implementing peer observation

Supervisors and administrators have an important role to play when implementing and encouraging peer observation. They can support teachers throughout the process in the following ways:

- Survey teachers in order to find out what kinds of support they might need for classroom observations (e.g., in terms of resources, administrative support, knowledge, and time).
- Gather resources on classroom observations such as articles or videotapes of classroom observations, and, if possible, invite outside experts or consultants to give a workshop on how to do observations.

- Ask teachers who have taken part in peer observation to explain what makes for a successful classroom observation.
- Where possible, free up time for teachers who want to engage in classroom observations.
- When teachers have successfully completed a series of classroom observations, encourage them to report to the other teachers about their experiences.

Summary

Peer observation can help teachers become more aware of the issues they confront in the classroom and how these can be resolved. Observation can also help narrow the gap between one's imagined view of teaching and what actually occurs in the classroom. By engaging in nonevaluative classroom observations, the responsibility of professional development can also shift from others (supervisors, peers, etc.) to the individual teacher. Because observation involves an intrusion into a colleague's classroom, procedures for carrying out observations need to be carefully negotiated between the participating parties. Having an observer in one's class is always something of a threatening experience because the teacher is now "on show." Assigning the observer a nonevaluative task goes some way toward minimizing the sense of threat, as does pairing teachers by choice and letting them negotiate the goals and procedures for observations.

Example of peer observation

Getting started

A group of beginning teachers in a language department requested assistance in professional development from their more experienced peers (Richards, 1998). They wanted evaluative feedback on their teaching but also wanted to combine this with feedback from their students. Therefore, a strategy of three-way observation was developed.

The process

The following strategy was implemented:

1. Pairs of new and experienced teachers decided to work together. The novice teacher invited a colleague to collaborate.

2. Each pair of teachers arranged to carry out several observations of each other's classes.
3. Data were collected at the end of each lesson on students', the teacher's, and the observer's perceptions of the lesson (different from usual peer observations). At the end of the lesson, the teacher allotted 5 to 7 minutes to the following activities:

The students were asked the following questions about the lesson:

Think back on the lesson that you just had and answer these questions.
1. What were the main goals of the lesson?
2. What is the most important thing you learned in the lesson?
3. What do you think was the most useful part of the lesson?
4. Was there anything about the lesson that was not very useful to you?

The observer was asked the following questions about the lesson:

As you observe the lesson, try to answer these questions.
1. What were the main goals of the lesson?
2. What is the most important thing the students learned in the lesson?
3. What do you think was the most useful part of the lesson?
4. Was there anything about the lesson that was not very successful?
5. How did you feel about the lesson as a whole?

The teacher was asked the following questions about the lesson:

At the end of the lesson you taught, answer these questions.
1. What were the main goals of the lesson?
2. What is the most important thing the students learned in the lesson?
3. What do you think was the most useful part of the lesson?
4. Was there anything about the lesson that was not very successful?
5. How do you feel about the lesson as a whole?

The outcome

The participants in this study found that:

- There was often closer agreement between the three sources of information on the goals of the lesson when it was taught by experienced teachers than when it was taught by inexperienced teachers.
- The experienced and inexperienced teachers differed on what they perceived as being the most successful part of a lesson. The experienced teachers judged a lesson successful in terms of what the learners were

likely to learn; the inexperienced teachers felt that a successful lesson was one that worked best from their point of view as a teacher.

Some insights

The most successful aspect of these classroom observations was that they allowed experienced teachers to serve as valued mentors to their less experienced colleagues. The fact that the experienced teachers were willing to go through the same process of critical reflection as the novice teachers gave them great credibility in the eyes of the novice teachers. Additionally, the experienced teachers became more thoughtful about their own teaching.

References and further reading

Cosh, J. (1999). Peer observation: A reflective model. *English Language Teaching Journal* 53(1), pp. 22–27.

Fitzpatrick, F. (1995). Peering at your peers. *Teacher Trainer* 9(2), p. 2.

Gebhard, J. G. (1996). *Teaching English as a foreign or second language*. Ann Arbor: University of Michigan Press.

Richards, J. C. (1998). *Teaching in action*. Alexandria, VA: TESOL.

Richards, J. C., & Lockhart, C. (1994). *Reflective teaching in second language classrooms*. New York: Cambridge University Press.

Wajnryb, R. (1992). *Classroom observation tasks*. Cambridge: Cambridge University Press.

Williams, M. (1989). A developmental view of classroom observation. *English Language Teaching Journal* 43(2), pp. 85–91.

Appendix

Checklist for monitoring a teacher's questioning strategies

Note (checkmark) how often the teacher asks the following questions at various intervals (for example, every 5 minutes) during the class.

Type of question asked	*Frequency*
1. *Factual/literal.* Teacher asks a question that the students can answer by reading or listening to the teacher.	_____
2. *Opinion/interpretative.* Teacher asks a question that the students can answer by "reading between the lines" from a text or from what the teacher says. Students can use own prior knowledge to answer.	_____

Type of response required   *Frequency*

1. *Display/fact.* Student must display his or her   _____
   knowledge of a topic by providing facts from
   memory.
2. *Referential/thought.* Student must provide an   _____
   answer that involves thought and reasoning in
   order to reach a logical conclusion.
3. *Choice.* Student must only provide a yes/no,   _____
   true/false answer – no explanation required.

Selection of student   *Frequency*

1. Calls student's name directly before asking   _____
   question.
2. Calls student's name directly after asking question.   _____
3. Calls for student volunteers after asking question.   _____
4. Allows students to self-select when to answer.   _____

7 Teaching portfolios

The nature of a teaching portfolio

A teaching portfolio is a collection of documents and other items that provides information about different aspects of a teacher's work. It serves to describe and document the teacher's performance, to facilitate professional development, and to provide a basis for reflection and review. Like many of the procedures described in this book, it is another form of teacher development that is built around self-appraisal and teacher-directed learning. Evans (1995, p. 11) characterizes the nature of a portfolio in the following way:

A professional portfolio is an evolving collection of carefully selected or composed professional thoughts, goals, and experiences that are threaded with reflection and self-assessment. It represents who you are, what you do, why you do it, where you have been, where you are, where you want to go, and how you plan on getting there.

A portfolio consists of a set of different types of documents and artifacts that have been selected on a principled basis (see below) and that are organized to tell a story. The collection is updated and revised when needed and is accompanied by the teacher's account of the rationale behind the collection. The portfolio can both serve as the basis for self-appraisal and be a component of the teacher's assessment.

Purpose and benefits of creating a portfolio

Teachers we have worked with find that a portfolio serves a number of purposes. First, it provides a demonstration of how a teacher approaches his or her work and presents evidence of the teacher's thinking, creativity, resourcefulness, and effectiveness. The portfolio can thus be submitted to a supervisor or manager as evidence of the standard of the teacher's performance.

Second, a portfolio serves as a source of review and reflection. The process of compiling the portfolio prompts the teacher to engage in a comprehensive self-assessment of different aspects of his or her work. By reviewing the portfolio (in consultation with a colleague or supervisor, if necessary), the teacher can make decisions about priorities and goals and areas for future development or improvement.

Third, a portfolio can promote collaboration with other teachers. For example, it can become part of the process of peer coaching (see Chapter 10); the peer reviews and discusses the portfolio and uses it to give feedback about the teacher's work. A particularly useful type of portfolio is one that is part of a team-teaching collaboration in which two teachers create a joint portfolio to accompany a class they both teach.

Working portfolio and showcase portfolio

There are two different types of portfolios, reflecting differences in their purpose and audience: a *working portfolio* and a *showcase portfolio*.

A working portfolio contains items that show how a teacher has progressed toward meeting a particular goal. For example, a teacher might decide he or she wants to move toward a more student-centered approach to learning. The portfolio contains documents and other items that provide evidence that this goal has been reached. Or a teacher might be trying to implement a genre-based approach (materials organized around genre types) in a writing course and the items in the portfolio are assembled in order to show how this has been achieved.

A showcase portfolio, as the name suggests, is designed to show the teacher at his or her best. Thus, it contains a collection of items that have been selected to show the range and depth of skills the teacher possesses. This kind of portfolio might be submitted as a part of an appraisal or included in an application for a new teaching position or for promotion. Teachers sometimes show us impressive portfolios of this kind. The following vignette shows how a teacher in Japan who is on a 2-year renewable contract is required to compile a showcase portfolio.

Vignette

Every faculty member at this university (in Japan) is required to submit a portfolio every 2 years for evaluation by an elected committee of faculty peers and the administration. The standards for this portfolio and its evaluation are outlined in detail in the university's Faculty Handbook. Specifically, the Faculty Review Committee (FRC) judges the responsiveness of candidates to problems in their teaching and their willingness to adapt teaching philosophies, styles, and strategies to the requirements of the university's program.

On the surface, it's very straightforward because the portfolio requirements and evaluation procedures are laid out in eight pages of text. The required materials for submission are: an updated curriculum vitae; a concise letter of self-evaluation of teaching, service, collegiality, and scholarship; highly selective samples of course materials demonstrating pedagogical approach, creativity, willingness to adjust to the educational needs of the students, and standards of judgment on student performance; and pertinent examples of scholarship. I soon discovered how difficult it is to create a high-quality portfolio of one's work. I have been fortunate to experience our process for showcase portfolios from both sides, as a candidate for reappointment and as a peer evaluator. The insights I have gained from reading dozens of my colleagues' portfolios, while sitting on the FRC four times, have certainly directed the composition of my own portfolios. My own painful experience of reading portfolios and trying to sort out what the materials were used for, why, and what the results were, led me to take extra care with the layout of my portfolio. Although I resent having to complete a portfolio every 2 years, each time I begin the process I quickly realize the benefits I receive from reflecting on my recent practices.

Tim Stewart

Reflection

- Why do you think it may be difficult to compile a quality teaching portfolio?
- What are some of the features of a teaching portfolio that appeal to you?

Two metaphors, the *mirror* and the *map*, summarize some of the benefits of assembling a teaching portfolio.

- *Mirror.* The mirror metaphor captures the reflective nature of a portfolio as it allows the teacher to view himself or herself over time. The portfolio contains samples of the teacher's work that illustrate a range of teaching skills and activities. It is usually created with a particular audience and purpose in mind. The focus is thus outward, toward other people, such as a colleague or supervisors. This influences the kinds of things that are included in the portfolio. The portfolio as mirror allows a teacher to reflect on his or her achievements as a teacher.

• *Map*. The map metaphor captures the idea of creating a plan and setting goals. After reviewing the evidence collected over time, the teacher can set immediate and longer-term goals. This is a process of review and self-assessment and deciding where one has arrived in one's development as a teacher and where one would like to go next. In this sense, the portfolio is like a map.

The following vignette from a teacher in the United States explains why he compiled a showcase portfolio, what he chose to include and why, and what he gained from this process.

Vignette

I have been teaching ESL/EFL/EAP for the past 20 years after having graduated with an M.A. At that time, teaching portfolios were not required, or even talked about. I knew what they were, but no one ever asked me for one, so I had never put one together. Recently, I've read more about them because, as an administrator, I have to find ways of assessing candidates for jobs with our program. I then read where teaching portfolios represent who a teacher is and what he or she has achieved over time. I decided that if I was going to be reading other people's portfolios, I should give this a go myself. I had wanted to see what I had done over the years in terms of teaching and other related work. I started to compile my teaching portfolio. Following what was suggested in the article I read and what suited me, I decided to include the following items:

1. Résumé
2. Letters of reference
3. Copies of transcripts
4. Copies of diplomas
5. Beliefs about my teaching
6. Course outlines
7. Student testimonials
8. Copies of materials I wrote
9. Student evaluations

I chose these nine items as I figured these would be an overall representation of who I am as a teacher. It took me about 3 months to put this portfolio together, but I am amazed at what I was able to assemble. I did not realize that I had accomplished so much, especially in the past few years. For example,

I had not realized the vast number of diverse courses I designed and taught successfully in the past few years. Additionally, I learned a lot from reading my student evaluations. For example, I was surprised to see some of them felt that they were not improving in their speaking and writing ability and that I was not correcting them enough. Apart from that, they all seemed satisfied that I was doing a good job. I understand their attitude toward corrections; it was as if they were thinking: "Why can't the teacher give me some magic feedback that will eliminate my writing problems?" I think I have to do a better job of explaining my strategies as a writing teacher. The most challenging aspect of the teaching portfolio for me was writing about my beliefs and values of teaching and learning. I found it very difficult to bring to the surface what I usually do instinctively when I teach. This was a major reflective essay for me, as I had to articulate beliefs that I have but that are not always easy to write down on paper. I really enjoyed putting my portfolio together. I was pleasantly surprised at the breadth and depth of what I have accomplished since I started teaching. Even though it was time-consuming, I hope others compile their teaching portfolios too.

Larry Zwier

Reflection

- Which other components could Larry have included in his portfolio?
- What would you like to include in a portfolio if you decided to assemble one?

As this example illustrates, compiling a teaching portfolio can be a very useful activity because it provides the opportunity to undertake a holistic assessment of one's teaching. It can also provide a rationale for undertaking some of the other activities discussed in this book, such as self-monitoring, journal writing, videotaping a lesson, and peer observation. Before starting a portfolio, however, teachers should be aware of some of the difficulties involved.

One of the most common difficulties reported is that of time (Wheeler, 1993). Assembling a portfolio takes a considerable amount of time and is best viewed as an ongoing long-term endeavor, with new features being added as needed and when they become available. Setting realistic goals and narrowing the contents of the portfolio are important, particularly at the outset. Deciding on the contents of the portfolio can also be problematic. If the portfolio is going to be part of a teacher's appraisal, then the purpose and contents of the portfolio should be discussed with the appraiser. When appraisal is not involved, discussion with a peer, with a mentor, or with other teachers who have developed portfolios is always helpful.

Nevertheless, we feel that a teaching portfolio can provide a useful opportunity for self-review and for collaboration with colleagues. In addition, a portfolio provides a richer picture of a teacher's strengths and accomplishments than a résumé would, and in the process of compiling the portfolio, goals for further professional development can be identified.

Procedures used in compiling a teaching portfolio

The purposes and audience for a portfolio are crucial in determining what is selected to go into it and how the contents of the portfolio are arranged. Many different kinds of items could be included in a teaching portfolio, but the contents should be selected carefully to ensure that they help create a coherent and effective portfolio and that they provide evidence of the teacher's competency, development, and self-awareness. A portfolio could include lesson plans, anecdotal records, student projects, class newsletters, videotapes, teacher evaluations, and letters of recommendation, but the form and contents of the portfolio will vary depending on its purpose.

An alternative to a paper-based portfolio is an electronic portfolio. An electronic portfolio has the same goals and content as a paper-and-pencil portfolio but presents them through the medium of the computer. It is a multimedia approach that allows the teacher to present the portfolio in a variety of formats, such as audio, video, graphics, and text. Hypermedia links are used to connect each section. The portfolio can be published on the Web and/or on a CD. Basic computer skills are needed, however, including the ability to create word-processing documents and incorporate computer graphics (Costantino & de Lorenzo, 2002).

Contents of a portfolio

The following are examples of the kinds of things that can be considered, though no more than eight to ten items would normally be included.

Evidence of your understanding of subject matter and current developments in language teaching
- A copy of your qualifications.
- A list of courses you have taken related to the areas you teach. For example, if you teach a course on speaking, you could include a list that includes such courses as Phonetics, Phonology, TESOL Methodology, and Second Language Acquisition Theory, to name a few.

- A critique of your school curriculum or languages program and its strengths and weakness. This could include comments on course outlines and tests.
- A critique or review (published or unpublished) of one or more books related to the subjects you teach. For example, if you teach a reading course, you might want to include a review of a book on the reading process and how to teach reading.
- A short essay describing your understanding of areas you teach (e.g., grammar, writing) and the principles you try to implement in your teaching.
- Written comments from a supervisor or colleagues on your expertise and knowledge in particular areas.

Evidence of your skills and competency as a language teacher
- A report by a colleague who visited your class
- Student evaluations
- Lesson plans
- Self-evaluations of lessons you have taught
- Examples of students' work
- A video (and/or audio) of one or more of your lessons
- A report by a supervisor, usually an evaluation
- Samples of assessment procedures you use with your students
- Examples of teaching materials you have prepared
- Photographs of you teaching your class
- Photographs of your classroom with students engaged in a learning activity
- Notes or cards of appreciation from past students
- Student achievements in outside examinations (such as the TOEFL test)
- Student placement success rate in university courses that require English

Your approach to classroom management and organization
- A description of your philosophy of classroom management
- A report by a colleague on how effectively you managed lessons your colleague observed
- Written comments on your management and organizational skills by a supervisor
- An account of critical incidents related to student behavior and how you responded to them
- An account of procedures used for teaching large classes and for using group work

- A video of one of your classes in session
- A diagram of your ideal language classroom
- A student account of your classroom management techniques and effectiveness

Documents showing your commitment to professional development
- A professional development plan for yourself
- A report on other teachers' classes that you have observed
- A report on any teacher group you belong to and your activities in relation to it
- A report on how you think you have developed since you began teaching
- An account of any classroom research you have conducted
- A list of courses and workshops you have taken in recent years
- A list of professional organizations you belong to (e.g., TESOL, IATEFL)
- A report on a conference or workshop you attended
- An annotated list of the books you have read in your area recently
- An account of some journal articles you have read
- A sample of any papers related to language teaching you have written recently for publication or otherwise

Information concerning your relationships with colleagues
- An account of ways in which you have assisted or mentored colleagues
- Letters from colleagues attesting to successful collaborations
- A report about the sense of collegiality you perceive in your school and where you fit in
- A report on ways you have contributed to your colleagues' professional development (e.g., did you present any brown-bag lunch seminars to your colleagues recently? If so, make a summary of this session).

The following vignette outlines an English language teacher's teaching philosophy, prepared for his teaching portfolio.

Vignette
I have a definite philosophy of teaching: I think that all students always come first. If a particular program (or course of action) will benefit them, I will endeavor to carry it out. If it's not going to benefit the students, I will scrap it or play it down. Pupils can learn well if they start liking the subject. To make the students like the subject, first, inject fun and humor; second,

relate it to real-life situations; third, give students a chance to pass in order to build up self-esteem; fourth, acknowledge effort and any improvement.

A teacher should be prepared to experiment with materials and teaching strategies because we don't know what actually works until we have tried different approaches and strategies. I put myself in the students' shoes and introduce to them whatever they could do to earn better grades – check for grammar in comprehension; teach them how to make inferences in comprehension and how to identify relevant points in summary writing.

Victor Ng

Reflection

- How would you characterize your philosophy of teaching?
- What sources do you think influenced the development of your teaching philosophy?

Organizing the contents of the portfolio

Portfolios usually contain a mix of teaching artifacts and written documents, grouped into different sections. As noted, we recommend including eight to ten items in a portfolio, depending on the amount of information included in each section.

The portfolio is not simply a set of documents, however. It is supported by the teacher's explanation of the goals, contents, and meaning of the portfolio as a whole and of the different items within it. This can be achieved through the following means (Costantino & de Lorenzo, 2002):

- *Introductions.* You should open your portfolio with an overview of the portfolio and the rationale for including the items in it. Each section of the portfolio usually contains its own introduction.
- *Artifacts.* Artifacts are the essential elements of a teaching portfolio and include such things as your philosophy of teaching, course outlines, unit and lesson plans, and other typical items.
- *Explanations.* These accompany each artifact in the portfolio and explain briefly what it is and why it is included. They may be a narrative text or simply a caption.
- *Reflections.* The value of a portfolio lies not merely in its contents, but in the meaning its contents have for you. This can be expressed through written reflections that accompany the different artifacts or sections within the portfolio.

- *Conclusion.* You should conclude your portfolio with a reflective essay or commentary in which you review the meaning of the portfolio for you.

The following vignette is an account of how an Australian teacher organized her teaching portfolio.

Vignette

I compiled my teaching portfolio and divided it into four main sections: "Qualifications and introduction," "Who I am as a teacher," "What I teach," and "My professionalism."

Qualifications and introduction

Who I am as a teacher
- My beliefs about my teaching – effective teaching and successful language learning

What I teach
- Sample course outlines
- A completed set of unit materials, including assessment tasks
- Sample lesson plans
- Samples of students' evaluations/feedback of lessons
- A videotape and/or audiotape of me teaching a class with a written description of what I was teaching and my reflection on that class
- Comments from colleagues
- My reflective journal

My professionalism
- My résumé
- My professional development plan (in point form)
- Research
- Copies of degrees, certificates, honors, and awards

Lyn May

Reflection

- What items in the categories mentioned here would you include in your teaching portfolio?
- How often do you think you should update your portfolio?

Implementing teaching portfolios

Compiling a teaching portfolio can be useful because it provides the opportunity to undertake a holistic assessment of one's teaching. By compiling a teaching portfolio, a teacher can assess his or her own progress and establish goals for professional development. Deciding on the audience for a portfolio (e.g., a working portfolio or a showcase portfolio) will help to determine what to include in it.

Portfolios have attracted increased interest as an institutional professional development strategy, often as a component of teacher appraisal. If the institution has opted for the use of portfolios, a number of questions need to be addressed.

1. Do teachers understand the nature and purpose of keeping a portfolio? An orientation session in which teachers are given the chance to examine examples of portfolios and discuss how they can be assembled is an important first step.
2. Participating teachers need to be given clear guidelines on what to include and within what time frame.
3. It is crucial to establish the criteria that will be used to assess the contents of a portfolio. Will assessment depend simply on assembling the agreed upon number of items, or will individual items also be assessed? Teachers need to know what they need to do in order to achieve a positive evaluation.

Summary

Compiling a teaching portfolio provides a teacher with an opportunity to document his or her strengths, skills, and accomplishments as a teacher and can also provide a rationale for undertaking some of the other activities discussed elsewhere in this book, such as self-monitoring, journal writing, videotaping a lesson, and peer observation. Assembling a portfolio is best viewed as an ongoing, long-term endeavor, with new features being added as needed and when they become available. Setting realistic goals and narrowing the contents of the portfolio are important, especially at the outset. The process of assembling the items to include in a portfolio can trigger self-appraisal, facilitate review, and help set goals for further development.

Example of a teaching portfolio

The following is an example of a small section of a teaching portfolio an EAP teacher in Singapore was required to compile by the school administration. This example explains how the teacher compiled his portfolio for part of one course he was teaching, Business and Technical Communication.

Teaching portfolio

BUSINESS AND TECHNICAL COMMUNICATION

PATRICK GALLO

Contents/Sections
1. Course outline and Web page files
2. Lecture notes
3. Tutorial materials
4. Continual assessment
5. Final assessment
6. Concluding remarks

This course folder includes course materials that I developed since I joined the course team in July 2001. Before each element presented in this folder, I have included a brief introductory paragraph that summarizes what is being presented and my comments on it. This folder highlights those aspects of the course that I had direct control over and those that I had the opportunity to shape with my colleagues into the form they currently take.

Section 1
  Course outline and Web page files
  1. Course objectives
  2. Course Web pages
     a. Calendar
     b. Lecture schedule
     c. Tutorial schedule
     d. Topics
     e. Staff contacts

Section 2
  Class notes
  1. Lecture 4: *Successful User Manual Writing 1* student handout
  2. Lecture 4: PowerPoint slides

3. Lecture 5: *Successful User Manual Writing 2* student handout
4. Lecture 5: PowerPoint slides
5. Mock Exam Workshop – User Manual Writing

Section 3
Tutorial materials
1. Sample textbook pages
2. Tutorial 4 and 5 guides (from textbook)
3. Lesson plans for each tutorial
4. Supplementary materials linked to various lessons

In July 2001, the course team had just finished their first edition of a course textbook, *Business and Technical Communication for IT Professionals*. This book served as our main text for 2001/2002. Consequently, the first tutorial guides and related assignments that I produced were based on this version of the user manual writing materials.

Section 4
Continual assessment
1. Pop quizzes for tutorials 4 and 5
2. User manual writing assignment sheets
3. User manual evaluation form

Section 5
Final assessment – user manual questions

Section 6
Concluding remarks

The preceding materials illustrate much of what I have been able to contribute to the course during the past 2 years. Perhaps from these materials you can see that I strive to organize each session I have with my students in a logical and efficient way. I care about presentation and the look of the materials we use. I use computer (and other) technologies and find ways to adapt existing activities into a multimedia environment. I do my best to maintain a spirit of unity with my colleagues who team teach this course with me, while injecting a breath of individuality into my lessons. On the other hand, the hard copies of handouts, lesson plans, and lecture notes do not provide a complete picture of what happens in my lectures or tutorials.

What may not be clear from these materials is my commitment to cooperative learning. In my lectures, and even more in my tutorials, I apply cooperative learning principles as much as I can. If you visit my class, you will see students constantly teaching one another or answering questions in pairs before displaying their knowledge to me and the whole class. I often apply Kagan's cooperative structures (cooperative learning methods) to the activities presented in the tutorials. Fortunately, before I arrived, many of the assignments were designed as group projects. Yet it is not enough to put students in a group and expect them to function appropriately. Cooperative skills must be explicitly taught and modeled during class. This is something I attempt to do during each tutorial session. Similarly, after group work, it is important to reflect on the process that the group has been through in order to learn what worked well and what could be improved upon for the next group project. Again, this is something I take the time to do in order to maximize my students' learning, not only of the specific writing and presentation skills we teach, but also of interpersonal communication skills and group-work strategies that will benefit them well beyond my classroom.

References and further reading

Anderson, R. S., & DeMulle, L. (1998). Portfolio use in twenty-four teacher education programs. *Teacher Education Quarterly* 25, pp. 23–31.

Antonek, J. L., McCormick, D. E., & Donato, R. (1997). The student teacher portfolio as autobiography: Developing a professional identity. *Modern Language Journal* 81, pp. 5–27.

Banfi, C. S. (2003). Portfolios: Integrating advanced language, academic, and professional skills. *English Language Teaching Journal* 57(1), pp. 34–42.

Barrett, H. C. (2000). Creating your own electronic portfolio: Using off-the-shelf software to showcase your own or student work. *Learning and Leading Technology* 27(7), pp. 14–21.

Brown, J. D., & Wolfe-Quintero, K. (1997). Teacher portfolios for evaluation: A great idea? Or a waste of time? *Language Teacher* 21(1), pp. 28–30.

Burke, K. (1997). *Designing professional portfolios for change.* Palatine, IL: IRI/SkyLight Training & Publishing.

Campbell, P., Cignetti, P., Melenyzer, D., Nettles, D., & Wyman, R. (1997). *How to develop a professional portfolio: A manual for teachers.* Boston: Allyn and Bacon.

Costantino, P., & De Lorenzo, M. N. (2002). *Developing a professional teaching portfolio.* Boston: Allyn and Bacon.

Evans, S. M. (1995). *Professional portfolios: Documenting and presenting performance excellence.* Virginia Beach, VA: Teacher's Little Secrets.

Green, J. E., & O'Sullivan Smyser, S. (1996). *The teacher portfolio: A strategy for professional development and evaluation.* Lancaster, PA: Technomic Publishing.

Lyons, Nona (Ed.). (1998). *With portfolio in hand: Validating the new teacher professionalism.* New York: Teachers College Press.

Martin-Kniep, G. (1998). *Why am I doing this? Purposeful teaching through portfolio assessment.* Portsmouth, NH: Heinemann.

Seldin, P. (1997). *The teaching portfolio.* Bolton: Anker Publishing.

Stone, B. A. (1998). Problems, pitfalls and benefits of portfolios. *Teacher Education Quarterly* 25, pp. 105–114.

Tanner, R., Longayroux, D., Beijaard, D., & Verloop, N. (2000). Piloting portfolios: Using portfolios in pre-service teacher education. *English Language Teaching Journal* 54(1), pp. 20–28.

Wheeler, P. H. (1993). *Using portfolios to assess teacher performance.* Livermore, CA: EREAPA Associates.

Wolfe, K., & Dietz, M. E. (1998). Teaching portfolios: Purposes and possibilities. *Teacher Education Quarterly* 25(1), pp. 9–22.

8 *Analyzing critical incidents*

The nature of critical incidents

A critical incident is an unplanned and unanticipated event that occurs during a lesson and that serves to trigger insights about some aspect of teaching and learning. Critical incident analysis in teaching involves the documentation and analysis of teaching incidents in order to learn from them and improve practice. The following vignette from a teacher in Japan is an example of a critical incident that occurred during a teacher's class.

Vignette

My students in a lower-intermediate listening/speaking class were assigned a pair activity. The first part of the lesson had focused on examples, working through the language needed. I gave them a handout, with clear step-by-step instructions. We had gone over the instructions on the handout, and I asked them if they understood what they were to do. I answered a few questions and the class started to work. I walked around to check that everyone was on track, and to answer any other questions. It looked like the pairs were off to a good start but, as I got to the back of the room, one pair asked, "Sir, what do you want us to do?"

Mark Wilkinson

Reflection

- What part of this incident made it "critical" for Mark?
- What do you think caused this incident?

This incident can be called a critical incident because it prompted the teacher to stop and reflect on the meaning of the event and perhaps to consider its longer-term implications. Documenting and reflecting on incidents of this kind can serve as an important part of the process by which teachers learn more about their teaching, their learners, and themselves.

An event becomes a critical incident depending on the way it is considered and the effects it has on one's understanding of teaching. It is the interpretation and meaning attributed to an incident that make it "critical." The majority of critical incidents that happen in classrooms are commonplace events that are critical in the sense that they reveal underlying beliefs or motives within the classroom. At first glance, these incidents may appear insignificant rather than critical, but they may become critical when they are subject to review and analysis. The following is an example from an American teacher.

Vignette

Recently, I had this student in an essay writing course. His name was Alfredo. The course involved students in writing 250–500-word essays. Alfredo was a good writer, and his essays were clearly better than those of the other students in the class. His grasp of sentence structure was excellent, he explained his ideas well through examples and details, and he organized his ideas effectively. I would read his essays and mark them with an "A," happy that there was such a good writer in the classroom – all of this while the other students were struggling with writing their essays, and indeed would often have to rewrite them to get a decent grade.

At the end of the semester, Alfredo told me one day, "If you had marked my essays lower, I would have worked harder." I was very surprised to get a remark like that from a student, and also upset to think that he felt he hadn't been pushed enough in my classroom, that he hadn't learned very much.

From this I learned that I couldn't judge students only by comparing them with the others – that I needed to judge them on their own terms. I needed to grade them in comparison with the work they were doing and were capable of doing. Otherwise, I wouldn't be doing these better students a favor – I wouldn't be helping them grow in their writing. Since then, I make sure that even if I think an essay is good, I give the student plenty of feedback as to what kind of changes or additions can be made to make the essay even better. I work with the students on not concentrating so much on grades, and concentrating more on their development as writers. I find that I am more relaxed in the writing classroom now, as the focus is more on the writing process, and not on simply putting marks on the final written product. So, I enjoy teaching writing much more now than before I got this comment from Alfredo.

Eric Harmsen

Reflection

- What made this incident "critical" for Eric?
- How did this incident change Eric's ideas about the role of feedback?

Critical incidents can be both positive and negative classroom events. They can be identified through reflecting on a "teaching high" or a "teaching low" (Thiel, 1999). A teaching high in a speaking class might be a spontaneous intervention or change in the lesson plan (i.e., an interactive decision) that had a positive effect on the lesson by increasing student participation. A teaching low might be a specific classroom incident that was immediately problematic and perplexing, such as reflecting on one student who suddenly stopped talking in a conversation activity for no apparent reason.

Purpose and benefits of analyzing critical incidents

Exploring critical incidents can have a number of benefits: It can serve as a form of reflective inquiry; it can help identify and resolve problems; it can serve to identify good practice; and it can give teachers a heightened sense of professional awareness. Collaborative discussion of critical incident reports allows for sharing of expertise, builds collegiality, and can help identify solutions to problems that may affect the institution. Writing about critical incidents can be a focus of activities such as journal writing, lesson reports, support groups, and peer coaching.

Analyzing critical incidents can facilitate professional development in a number of ways.

- *It can create a greater level of self-awareness.* By writing about and discussing critical incidents, a teacher can become more aware of some of his or her assumptions about language teaching and learning. The following vignette shows how a teacher became aware of differences in American and Korean classroom cultures.

Vignette

One day a student raised her hand and asked if she was allowed to use Korean during the class. I realized that when the student sought permission to speak her native language in class, it raised a conflict with my belief system about what education should be about. My background in the United States led me to assume that all students could lead autonomous lives within the school in that they are responsible for their own actions. I said that it was up to her if she wanted to clarify something with a friend during the class.

Eric Harmsen

Reflection

- In what way does this incident reveal differences in classroom cultures?
- What do you think Eric learned from reflecting on this critical incident?

- *It can prompt an evaluation of established routines and procedures.* By reflecting on how students respond to different teaching techniques and strategies, the teacher can fine-tune his or her instructional repertoire.

Vignette

One day when I was teaching I realized that when I ask EFL students questions, I am actually asking them to perform a complicated task. It was when I was teaching a class and a student misspelled the word *promote* during a dictation exercise. After he corrected it, I asked him if he understood the word. He said he knew the word, but he couldn't hear it in the sentence that I had just read. This experience showed me again that listening to directions is not an easy task for an EFL student. That day after that incident and after I had written it in my journal, I realized that when I ask for an understanding response from my EFL students, I am asking them to do much more than just give an understanding response. I now realize that my EFL students must go through three steps, not just one step, to give an answer in a language that is foreign to them. First, they must listen and understand the language. Next, after they perform the first task of listening, they must understand the directions for the activity, or how to do the activity. Finally, they must choose and organize the appropriate words in the foreign language to express the understanding response—really more complicated than I had imagined.

Jane Hoelker

Reflection

- How do you think Jane benefited from writing about this critical incident?

- *It can encourage teachers to pose critical questions about teaching.* By considering the meaning of critical incidents, teachers learn to pose questions about many dimensions of teaching that they had not given a great deal of thought to.
- *It can help bring beliefs to the level of awareness.* By writing, reading, analyzing, and interpreting critical incidents, teachers can become more aware of their beliefs and decide if any of them should be changed. Kagan (1992) points out that teachers' beliefs are generally stable and determine the kind of instruction teachers provide to students. However, beliefs are generally not open to critical examination. Analyzing critical incidents is one way that beliefs can be clarified and explored.
- *It can create opportunities for action research.* Critical incident analysis can be the starting point for follow-up research, such as a case study (Chapter 9) or action research (Chapter 12). The example near the end of this chapter describes how a critical incident turned into an action research project for a teacher.
- *It can help build a community of critical practitioners.* Through examining critical incidents with other teachers, a community of practitioners can be created who may be able to influence teaching practices and policies in a school.
- *It can provide a resource for teachers.* Compiling a file of critical incident reports can serve as a useful resource for both new teachers and experienced teachers.

Procedures used for analyzing critical incidents

Anatomy of a critical incident

Critical incidents can reveal some of the underlying principles, beliefs, and assumptions that shape classroom practices. Tripp (1993) suggests that there are two stages to understanding a critical incident: The first stage is to describe the incident, and the second is to explain its meaning (the "what" and the "why"). The incident becomes a critical incident when it is viewed in terms of something that has significance in a wider context. Figure 8.1 gives an example of this process.

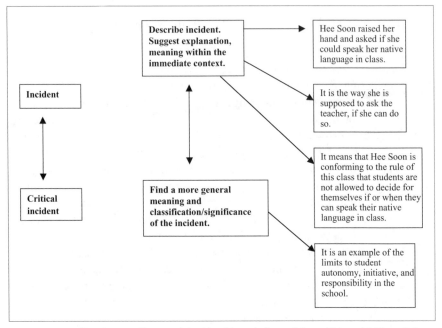

Figure 8.1: Understanding a critical incident (adapted from Tripp, 1993, p. 26).

Preparing and analyzing critical incident reports

When using critical incidents as a professional development activity, a teacher or a group of teachers would normally plan to monitor their teaching for a specific period of time (e.g., one term or for the duration of a particular course) and prepare a series of incident reports. These can then be shared and serve as a basis for discussion and review.

Many critical incidents are typical accounts of commonplace classroom events that one ascribes critical significance to. Thiel (1999) suggests that the reporting of such critical incidents (written or spoken) should follow specific steps: self-observation, describing what happened, self-awareness, self-evaluation.

- *Self-observation.* The first step in the analysis of a critical incident can be accomplished by identifying significant events that occur in the classroom through observing one's own teaching. Documenting such events can be accomplished by keeping a teaching journal, by making an audio or video recording, or by preparing a lesson transcript or a lesson report of the relevant part of the lesson. If the teacher is participating in a collaborative activity such as peer observation, the two teachers can try to recall critical incidents that may have occurred during the lesson. The following vignette describes an incident from a teacher's class in Malaysia.

Vignette

On the first day of class, I went in to teach a 2-hour composition class. I decided to get them to write a short essay about themselves in order to test their writing ability. Half of the students managed to finish a few paragraphs after 1 hour, while the other half could not even start one sentence. They looked very frustrated and I really did not know what to do with the ones who finished first and could not leave the class. I never realized I would get one class with so many different proficiency levels to deal with. I just kept thinking: "My M.A. did not really prepare me for such situations."

Mary Ellis

Reflection

- What do you think Mary learned from this critical incident?
- How would you advise Mary to handle this situation?

- *Describing what happened.* The second step in reporting critical incidents involves writing a detailed description of what happened. This description should include details of *the incident itself, what led up to it,* and *what followed.*
- *Self-awareness.* The third step in reporting a critical incident can be accomplished by analyzing why the incident happened. It may be necessary to look at the whole picture of the classroom lesson, the lesson objectives, the students, the disposition of the students, the time of day, the mode of delivery of the lesson, and so on, as there are rarely easy, single cause-and-effect explanations as to why a critical incident occurred during a lesson.

- *Self-evaluation.* The final step in reporting critical incidents is probably the most difficult. At this stage, the teacher considers how the incident itself led to a change in his or her understanding of teaching.

In reflecting on a critical incident, specific questions the teacher can ask (or that can be posed by a collaborating teacher) include the following:

- Why was this incident significant to you?
- What happened directly before the event?
- What happened directly after the event?
- How did you react at the time of the event?
- What is your interpretation of this event?
- What underlying assumptions about your teaching does this critical incident raise for you?
- Now that you have reflected on this critical incident, would you react any differently if it happened again? Why or why not?

The emphasis here is reflecting on the incident in terms of its personal meaning. This may mean examining one's beliefs and understandings and how these make the incident critical. One way of developing insights into critical incidents is to collect data on lesson breakdowns (Thiel, 1999; Wajnryb, 1992). Wajnryb (1992, p. 87) suggests that a lesson breakdown is "a point in a lesson when, due to a communication problem or misunderstanding, the lesson is unable to proceed." The teacher describes the point in the lesson where the breakdown occurred and asks why it happened. He or she then reflects on how it was or was not resolved. If it was resolved, how this happened can be documented and discussed. If it was not resolved, ways in which it could have been resolved are suggested.

Personal critical incidents

Although most critical incidents are likely to be events that have occurred in the classroom and/or school, some may result in a significant change in a teacher's personal, as well as professional, life. For example, a teacher might have been so inspired or challenged by participating in a conference or workshop that he or she decided to return to graduate school in order to learn more about teaching. The following critical incident would be viewed as an event that resulted in a momentous personal change, which signaled a significant point in the teacher's professional development.

Vignette

I was talking to some fellow younger teachers after class one day in the coffee shop, and in came other, older (longer service at the school) teachers from the school. I was not enjoying myself teaching because I was forced to use a particular method of teaching composition, and the school advertised itself as a proud user of this method. As I had no teaching qualifications (I had a B.A. in music), I had thought that I would benefit from having a structured approach to teaching. However, 9 months into the job I was bored and frustrated with this so-called method because I was not allowed to really talk and interact with the students (I did after class, but I had little time for this as my teaching hours increased). I found that I really enjoyed the classroom and "teaching" and the students, but I was having a great deal of difficulty following the method the school was forcing me to teach. Then that afternoon, when the "older" teachers came in and sat with us, I asked them about their feelings about this method and my frustrations. They replied that I was stupid to worry about the method as one did not have to prepare because everything was prepared for the teacher in the book. They just laughed at me and said that I would get used to it and just come to class and "plug into" the system as they had been doing for the past 3 to 5 years. At that moment, my life flashed before me and I saw myself as a similar cynical language teacher just plugging into a system. I decided there and then to go back to graduate school and get a qualification in language teaching and avoid language schools that pushed any one method over a teacher's choice.

Harold Bennet

Reflection

- What makes this critical incident an epiphany of sorts for Harold?
- What critical moments have you experienced in your professional life? your life? What prompted them?

Many teachers find that they can make connections and better understand their work by reflecting on critical incidents in their professional life. The value of biographical data has been recognized when discussing how teachers develop their understanding of teaching and of themselves. Freeman (1996, p. 89) has pointed out that it is necessary for teachers to put themselves at the center of telling their life stories, and this, he says, follows a jazz maxim: "You have to know the story in order to tell the story." When reflecting on critical incidents within one's teaching career, answers to the following questions might be sought (Bartlett, 1990):

- Why did I become a language teacher?
- Do these reasons still exist for me now?

- How has my background shaped the way I teach?
- What does it mean to be a language teacher?
- Is the teacher I am the person I am?
- What is my philosophy of language teaching?
- Where did this philosophy come from?
- How was this philosophy shaped?
- What are my beliefs about language learning?
- What critical incidents in my training to be a teacher shaped me as a teacher?
- Do I teach in reaction to these?
- What critical incidents in my career shaped me as a teacher?
- Do I teach in reaction to these critical incidents?

Implementing critical incident analysis

As with other activities that involve writing about teaching, a number of decisions need to be made in carrying out critical incident analysis. These include the following:

- *Who is the audience for the analysis?* Audiences might include the teacher, other teachers (e.g., in a discussion group), or a supervisor.
- *What kinds of incidents are useful to write about?* You can choose either to write about whatever kinds of incidents occur or to focus on particular kinds of incidents, depending on your goals. If you make critical incident analysis the focus of a discussion group, you might choose to focus on particular kinds of incidents (e.g., those relating to classroom management, teaching strategies, or learning styles). The group then meets from time to time to discuss and reflect on the incidents its members have experienced.
- *How much time will it take?* One of the drawbacks of analyzing critical incidents is finding time to write down an incident after the class. One way to counteract this is to talk into a recorder directly after the incident or class, and write it out later from reflection. This way, none of the details will be omitted because of time or fatigue constraints directly after class.

Summary

Critical incidents are unplanned incidents that occur during teaching and that serve to trigger insights about teaching. Critical incident analysis involves documenting and reflecting on such incidents, whether as an individual or in a collaborative activity. Although it can be an activity for it own sake, it is best to combine one or more activity, such as journal writing or creating a teaching portfolio, when analyzing critical incidents.

Example of a critical incident

The following summary of a critical incident appears in a collection of cases of critical incidents and teaching dilemmas (Richards, 1998). This collection contains seventy-six examples of significant teaching incidents and how the teachers responded to them, as reported by the teachers themselves. These examples provide excellent examples about how writing about critical incidents can help teachers think about critical issues relevant to their teaching, help them frame these issues, and show different ways in which teachers draw on experience, beliefs, and pedagogical knowledge as they respond to these issues. The incidents in the collection are described in a three-part format:

- *Context*. Where the teacher is working
- *Problem*. A description of the incident
- *Solution/response*. How the teacher responded to the incident

Critical incident

This incident arose from a teacher's attempts to help students remember new vocabulary (Laurie, 1998, pp. 360–364).

Difficulties in learning new vocabulary in a one-to-one tutorial

CONTEXT

Roz was teaching in a private language school in London. She was teaching a private tutorial in order to expand the student's vocabulary, improve accuracy of the student's basic grammar, and practice reading, speaking, and general conversation. The student also wanted to continue learning phonemic script. One week into the program, the student wanted specific vocabulary and readings relevant to the fashion industry. Roz used visual aids, mime and physical actions, and role-plays and simulations but did not use audiotapes or videotapes.

PROBLEM

One day Roz noticed that J (the student) had difficulty remembering newly presented vocabulary – eight to ten items. This surprised Roz for the following reasons: J is a highly motivated student, Roz uses aids to enhance memory, J has a good general knowledge of English, and J is extroverted and highly motivated to communicate in English. It seemed illogical to Roz that J should have such difficulty remembering new vocabulary related to a subject of great interest to her.

SOLUTION/RESPONSE

As a result of this critical incident, Roz devised two simple and compatible strategies as solutions. The first was to restrict the number of items she presented and to increase their recycling frequency. She persisted with the same method of presentation, practice, and performance in all three lessons that followed. The second was to incorporate sensory aids into the lesson in greater variety and quantity. Roz collected twelve to fifteen visual aids from fashion magazines from which she drew up a list of twenty relevant words with an adjoining jumbled list of the same words in the phonemic script. These two lists formed the lexical basis of the three lessons.

At the beginning of each lesson, Roz asked J to highlight any words she knew or was familiar with. She could not do this in the first lesson, but in the following two lessons she was able to recognize and highlight items from the previous lessons. With a high frequency of recycling and backtracking, J's inaccuracies decreased considerably, which made the hard work worthwhile, according to Roz.

References and further reading

Bartlett, L. (1990). Teacher development through reflective teaching. In J. C. Richards & Nunan, D. (Eds.), *Second language teacher education* (pp. 202–214). New York: Cambridge University Press.

Brislin, R. W., Cushnew, K., Cherrie, C., & Young, M. (1986). *Intercultural interactions: A practical guide*. Beverly Hills, CA: Sage.

Brookfield, S. D. (1990). *The skillful teacher*. San Fransciso: Jossey-Bass.

Cortazzi, M. (1994). State-of-the-art article: Narrative Analysis. *Language Teaching* 27, pp. 156–170.

Freeman, D. (1996). Redefining research and what teachers know. In K. Bailey & D. Nunan (Eds.), *Voices from the language classroom* (pp. 88–115). New York: Cambridge University Press.

Kagan, D. M. (1992). Implications of research on teacher belief. *Educational Psychologist* 27, pp. 65–90.

Lortie, D. (1975). *Schoolteacher*. Chicago: University of Chicago Press.

Nespor, J. (1987). The role of beliefs in the practice of teaching. *Journal of Curriculum Studies* 19, pp. 317–328.

Richards, J. C. (1998). *Teaching in action*. Alexandria, VA: TESOL.

Thiel, T. (1999). Reflections on critical incidents. *Prospect* 14(1), pp. 44–52.

Tripp, D. (1993). *Critical incidents in teaching*. London: Routledge.

Wajnryb, R. (1992). *Classroom observation tasks*. Cambridge: Cambridge University Press.

9 Case analysis

The nature of case analysis

Case analysis in teacher education involves collecting information over time about a teaching situation and using that information to help better understand the situation and to derive principles from it. In language teaching and other fields, it is based on the use of accounts (case studies) of how practitioners carry out their practice and resolve the issues that they confront. Case analysis has a long history in fields such as business, law, and medicine. In business education, for example, students might study a real-world example of a successful business venture and try to determine the principles that accounted for its success. The Harvard Law School has used case studies since 1870 (Carter & Unklesbay, 1989), but the case method of teaching did not enter into the field of education until much later. In fact, it was not until the mid-1980s that any literature was published on cases (Shulman, 1992), although vignettes, critical incidents, and classroom simulations have been used for some time to help novice teachers cope with their first years in the classroom (Kagan, 1993). In 1986, the Carnegie Task Force on Teaching as a Profession suggested that case methodology should be more widely used in teacher education courses: "Teaching 'cases' illustrating a great variety of teaching problems should be developed as a major focus of instruction" (1986, p. 76). In language teaching, a number of collections of cases have been published in recent years (e.g., Richards, 1998, and the TESOL Case Study series).

In order to understand what a case is, consider the issue of classroom management and how we could learn more about the principles of good classroom management. One approach would be to consult a textbook on teaching and find out what information it contained. Such information would probably be a summary of the opinions of experts and practitioners. An alternative approach would be to visit the classroom of a teacher who had excellent classroom management skills in order to find out how the teacher achieved these results. We could, for example, ask the teacher to videotape his or her class and then view the tape later, noting the instances of good classroom management. We could also ask the teacher to comment on what he or she was doing while watching the tape and what the teacher's overall methods of managing the class were. Additionally, we could ask the teacher to focus on and document over time some instances of how various situations that occurred during class were successfully managed. This written summary is known as a case. We (or others) could then read and analyze the case in order to understand the principles the teacher made use of in managing the class, as well as some of the more general issues involved in classroom management. The following vignette is an example of how two teachers in the United Arab Emirates decided to find out why two EFL students were such good writers.

Vignette

My colleague, Awil Hashi, and I decided to investigate why two EFL students were successful writers. We developed the following case study of both writers. First some background: Both were from a non-English-medium, government-directed school system. Ms. A achieved 500 on the TOEFL examination within 10 months of entering level four, and Ms. N within 12 months. Most students take 18 to 24 months to get 500 on the TOEFL! So, we wondered if the context would highlight and isolate factors such as student motivation, aptitude, diligence, and resourcefulness that would encourage writing expertise in their L2.

First, we wanted to back up our intuitions that they were good writers. To do this I performed a T-unit analysis (count the average number of words per main clause) on the language in the 10 (Ms. N) to 14 (Ms. A) writing assignments they had produced; the results supported our intuition that the students were mastering the written syntax of English at a rapid pace. They also surprised us by using subordinate clauses correctly 100% of the time (i.e., adverbial, noun, and especially relative clauses). So, this is evidence that they really are good writers.

Next, we conducted e-interviews and face-to-face interviews. We looked at different strategies (Kind of Learner, Learning Style, Left Brain and Right Brain, and Motivating Yourself and Setting Goals) for the content of the e-interviews. My colleague and I were impressed at their awareness of meta-cognition! Ms. A stated that her uncles were her role models, all six of whom have graduated from a university! This extrinsic motivation pushes her to learn English in order to graduate from Zayed University and pursue a career in science. Ms. N saves sentences to use in writing dialogues that she imagines between characters. She is more extroverted than Ms. A and likes to listen to dialogues in movies. She likes to listen to English songs as much as Arabic songs, and from when she was young she told herself that she wanted to be a good English speaker. Her family is the source of her extrinsic motivation; they give her the power and they push her, she says.

Jane Hoelker and Awil Hashi

Reflection

- What do you think can be learned from conducting case studies of exceptional learners?
- How far do you think one can generalize from information obtained from a case study?

This example of a case study illustrates a number of characteristics of a case:

- It focuses on collecting information about a real-life situation that can be used to discuss a problematic issue in teaching.
- It focuses on an instance or example of something we wish to learn more about.
- It has implications beyond the situation described.
- It can be an instructive example for other teachers.
- It involves a detailed description of a situation but does not necessarily analyze or interpret it. The case thus becomes the data for analysis and interpretation by the reader.

The following kinds of case studies have been found useful as part of a teacher development initiative:

- Information collected over a period of a semester concerning how two different students (one with high proficiency and one with low proficiency) performed during group activities
- An account of the problems a teacher experienced during his or her first few months of teaching
- An account of how two teachers implemented a team-teaching strategy and the difficulties they encountered
- An account of observation of one high-achieving student and one low-achieving student over a semester in order to compare their patterns of classroom participation
- A journal account of all of the classroom management problems a teacher had to deal with in a typical school week

- An account of how a teacher made use of lesson plans over a 3-week period
- An account of how two colleagues resolved a misunderstanding that occurred between them in relation to the goals of a course
- A description of all the changes a student made in a composition she was working on over a 3-week period, from the drafting stage to the final stage

The following vignette illustrates how an ESL teacher dealt with problems foreign students were experiencing in their first semester at an English-medium university.

Vignette

Many of the foreign students who come to the university where I teach tell me that they have a difficult time adapting to the new environment. However, when I ask them specifically what the problems are, their answers are usually vague. So, this past semester I asked them to keep a journal in which they described the various problems they think they experienced each week. We agreed to meet together once a week to review their findings. We kept this schedule going for about 5 weeks and compiled a list of problems (e.g., language, cross-cultural misunderstandings) and the places they occurred (e.g., in lectures, in meetings). I found this a useful source of information that could be very useful for the university and the students found it a great way to focus on problems that were real and that they could reflect on now that they were written. The weekly discussions involved not only reviewing the problems but also attempting to generate solutions to them (some successful, others less successful).

Peter Claffey

Reflection

- What types of problems do you think foreign students experience in an English-medium university in a foreign country?
- How could Peter have conducted his case study in a different way?

A case is different from a critical incident in that it starts from identification of a particular issue or phenomenon and then selects a method for collecting information about it. Critical incident analysis involves looking back on an unplanned classroom incident and reflecting on its meaning. A case study usually has a broader focus than a critical incident, though a critical incident can provide the initial motivation for a case study. A case is thus a narrative description of a real-life situation, a "slice of life," that can provide a forum for teachers to explore issues that arise in real classrooms.

Purpose and benefits of using cases

Analyzing cases based on descriptions of how teachers deal with issues encountered in the classroom can provide a basis for arriving at valuable insights and principles, enabling teachers to verbalize and share the problem-solving strategies they make use of in their teaching. The case reports can also be a valuable resource for other teachers, particularly less experienced teachers. A collection of cases focusing on a particular kind of problem or issue (e.g., teaching beginning students, dealing with reluctant learners, teaching vocabulary from newspaper resources) can be a valuable teacher-training resource for novice teachers. The following vignette is an example of a case study that was carried out by two primary school teachers in Australia.

Vignette

We were interested in learning more about the learning strategies used by our students. We felt that we needed to know more about the strategies used by successful learners in our ESL classes. We also wanted to find out how the learners were responding to our teaching. The following questions were used to guide our investigation:

- What learning strategies are used by good language learners in our classes?
- Do our learners use English outside of the classroom?
- Do they feel good about learning English?

We identified two children, both age seven, whom we believed were good language learners. We chose these two learners because they seemed to be learning English more successfully in the class. We decided to collect information on them from classroom observation, learner journals, and interviews. We planned to observe the learners over a term. From classroom observation, we built up examples of our learners doing the following:

- Listening attentively
- Asking questions
- Using the target language both in and outside of the classroom

- Interacting with others in English
- Volunteering answers
- Using resources such as dictionaries

We also interviewed the students to find out what they found easy, enjoyable, interesting, or difficult in particular activities and why. The students also kept journals in which they wrote about their feelings and attitudes toward language learning. In looking over the data, we found that our students used a variety of strategies to help them become successful language learners. For example, we asked, "How do you remember what you've learned?" Answers included:

- It's easy to remember when you listen.
- I do it over and over again.
- I practice with friends and family.
- I write things down I want to remember.
- I stick sentences on my wall in my room.
- I spend lots of time going over my book because I like it and I learn. I would still study if my teacher didn't see it or mark it.

Even though we didn't learn anything surprising from our investigation, it was useful to confirm and make explicit some things that we knew intuitively. We learned a useful strategy to more effectively facilitate our students' learning. The strategy involves asking the following questions:

- How did you go about doing this?
- Which way of doing this works best for you?

I. Zordana and S. Bojanic

Reflection

- How do you think the teachers might make use of the information they obtained?
- Can you think of other reasons to account for the children's success in learning English?

Procedures for analyzing and discussing cases

Sources for cases

There are two sources for cases. Cases can be based on what happens in a teacher's own classroom. By writing and reflecting on their own cases, teachers can better arrive at an understanding of the events as they un-fold. As Olshtain and Irit (1998, p.187) maintain, writing and reflecting on cases allows teachers "to impose order and coherence on the unpredictable classroom reality where there are always alternative solutions to cope with similar problems." Teachers can also read and discuss cases prepared by other teachers. These can be used as the basis for group discussions. The following vignette explains the focus of a case study of a teacher at a tertiary institution in Malaysia.

Vignette

I encountered this situation initially with one of my composition classes. One day just toward the end of the class on peer response, Rizal did not feel that comments made by his peer, Khairul, were worthwhile and he made a sudden outburst and shouted that peer-editing was a waste of time. This situation had never happened in my class before. When the class period ended, I wondered if this was the feeling of some of the other students who weren't voicing their opinions. (Malay students are generally very polite and don't want to offend their teachers.) As peer-editing was an integral part of my writing classes, it couldn't be dropped (the curriculum had to be followed for students to get credit. Also, classes were monitored by the English department from the U.S. university they were twinning with), so I decided to turn the initial critical incident into a case that I could focus on and reflect on, and so I decided to monitor the students' use of peer-editing over a whole semester to find out how they made use of it and how useful it was.

Mary Ellis

Reflection

- How do you think Mary could collect the information she needs for her case study?
- If she only had time to focus on two or three students in the class, how do you think she should decide which students to focus on in her case study?

Finding a topic for a case

In our experience, when thinking about possible topics for case reports, it is important to keep in mind two aspects of cases.

- They describe a teaching situation, event, or episode that will be the focus of reflection and analysis.
- The report or description allows for generalizations to be made from it or for a principle to be derived from it.

If a description of an event does not have any significance beyond itself and does not lead to any meaningful or relevant conclusion, it is merely an anecdote and does not justify detailed analysis and reflection. A topic or issue for a case report should be chosen, therefore, on the expectation that something worthwhile and significant can be learned from it. Topics for case reports can be identified by focusing on a particular *issue* or *problem*. For example:

- A dilemma that occurred within a lesson
- A classroom routine or activity you find problematic
- A learner behavior that causes problems in lessons
- A misunderstanding that occurred between a teacher and a colleague or a teacher and students in a class

The following vignette illustrates how a teacher checked how her students used their dictionaries throughout the semester.

Vignette

I teach EAP language students from China who are getting ready to enter university in Singapore. I was curious how the students used their dictionaries during the semester because I noticed that they used them a lot and they never went anywhere without them. Some had electronic dictionaries, but most of them had the usual book-type dictionaries. So I decided to ask the students to keep an account of several aspects concerning their use of their dictionaries. Specifically, I asked them to write in a journal how often they used their dictionary each day during a 1-week period, what words they looked up (I asked them to write down all these words for a 1-week period), and generally how much time they spent using the dictionary during that 1-week period. I chose three students whom I could depend on (each had a different proficiency level—high, medium, low) and I told them that I would give them a detailed report and analysis of their usage of the dictionary if they helped me with this. I was astonished at what I found. Regardless of their proficiency level, all three used the dictionary most days of the week and wrote down more than 100 words each. It was a real eye-opener for me, and now I realize how important the dictionary is for these students. I think we teachers must rethink their place in the EAP program.

Mary Ellis

Reflection

- What particular issue would you focus a case study on in your context?
- What other means could Mary have used to check her students' use of dictionaries?

Topics for case reports can also be identified by focusing on a particular *part of a lesson* that is problematic or of special interest. For example:

- The opening stage of a lesson
- Setting up an activity
- Dealing with transitions between activities
- Closing a lesson

These topics can also be identified by focusing on a particular *type of teaching activity*. For example:

- A grammar activity
- A vocabulary activity
- A pronunciation activity

The following vignette illustrates how a language teacher focused on her students' pronunciation problems.

Vignette

I had noticed that many of my students had some real problems with their pronunciation and I decided to give them some extra classes to try to help them practice speaking while focusing specifically on pronunciation, rather than interrupt the regular class activities, and to monitor their improvements in pronunciation over a term. Before implementing a new teaching strategy with the whole class, I decided to try it out with three of the students over a term and to use them as a kind of case study. So I asked the three students who exhibited the most serious problems (I could not understand their answers in class) if they would like to practice with me after the regular classes, and they agreed. I came up with the following activity for these exercises: I gave them a reading aloud activity each week for 6 weeks (one term in our school). I also gave them some pronunciation exercises to do at home. I recorded their performance and noted their progress. First, I noted their initial pronunciation problems and developed a log for each of the three students. After the term ended, I noted what sounds improved and what sounds needed continued practice. Some of the sounds in each of the three students' pronunciation really did improve with this activity, but some did not. So I am going to target the problematic sounds in a different way and see if it helps. Anyway, I think it was a worthwhile activity and my students were really appreciative of the extra time I took with them.

Mark Wilkinson

Reflection

- What do you do to help students improve their pronunciation?
- What other activities might Mark have attempted to improve his students' pronunciation?

Writing case studies

We suggest that a written case analysis include a description of the context, an outline of the problem/issue, and an account of the solutions that were implemented. The writer starts with an introduction to a *setting*, introduces a particular *dilemma/problem*, outlines the dilemma/problem and what the *consequences* of the dilemma/problem were, and adds a *conclusion* in which an attempt is made to derive principles or to solve the dilemma/problem.

The following vignette is a summary of a case in which a course coordinator tried to implement changes in an EFL program in Korea (Farrell, 1998, pp. 125–128). The case is summarized and in the words of the author, who was the course coordinator; it includes the context, the problem, and a solution.

Vignette

Context
- Small women's university in Seoul, South Korea.
- Program had twenty-five part-time native Korean English instructors.

- Syllabus was designed exclusively by the director, as were all the examinations.
- Each freshman and sophomore student had to take English classes: conversation and video/audio classes for freshmen, and reading classes (prescribed text) for sophomore students.

Problem

- Because I was the first foreign director of the program, the instructors did not know what to expect.
- Previous teacher meetings consisted of giving the instructors their syllabi.
- Needs analysis had never been conducted.
- The instructors had not had any meetings during the semester or year to discuss their classes.
- What developed: Different groups of teachers (usually arranged by age) gathered informally and discussed things about their work at lunch or in the teachers' lounge.
- Instructors never participated in other group discussions.
- I tried to establish better collaboration by having more teacher meetings on topics, usually topics I had thought important.
- Everybody came to these meetings, and at first I was pleased.
- However, it soon became apparent that I was doing all of the talking at the meetings, even when we broke up into group discussions.
- When I tried to institute peer observation, I was indirectly told, "This is not the Korean way," or "It will not work." And indeed it did not. The biggest obstacle I faced was that as a director in a Korean situation, I should have been seen as acting more authoritatively (as one professor later remarked).
- I was never given feedback from the teachers during my first year as director; instead, they gave feedback to the previous director, who in turn told me everything was great.
- I knew better.

Solution/Response

- To solve this dilemma, I tried a few different methods, some of which succeeded while others were only marginally successful.
- I tried to meet the teachers "by chance," outside my office, to see who would be interested in talking about teaching and who might be interested in sharing their views about the program.
- About teaching: Teachers could bring lesson plans (their favorite ones) and put them in a drawer. Both old and new teachers could compare and use them. What really happened was that I put in my lesson plans.

Some other teachers did the same, but only a few, and the drawer did not fill up. But I did manage to tap into some of the informal discussions.

- About the program: I started an examination committee. This method seemed to work because the teachers had a vested interest in that their students were going to take these examinations. If Korean teachers have one overriding concern, it is for their students' success.
- Surprise: From this examination committee, I found a group of teachers who were interested in the program and their own teacher development. These five teachers met with me regularly to discuss their classroom situations in more detail. We taped our classes and brought these tapes to our group meetings. We played the tapes and discussed our teaching. These meetings continued throughout the semester.

Tom Farrell

Reflection

- What are some of the main issues that emerged from this case study?
- What other responses could have been made to the problems Tom encountered?

Using case studies

The purpose of a case is to serve as input for discussion and reflection. This can be done in a variety of ways. For example, teachers in a school might decide to write a case analysis based on a class they share (e.g., a TOEFL prep class). The cases can be used in the following way:

- The case reports can be circulated for comment and discussion and later put into a file cabinet in the teachers' resource room for others to read.
- They can be circulated among a group of teachers who can read them and comment on them.
- They can be circulated by e-mail to a teacher's group.
- They can be reviewed in group sessions (see Chapter 4) using a set of questions to guide the review process. For example, the following questions are "intended to encourage creative and critical thinking, rather than suggest predetermined views about cases" (Jackson, 1997, p. 7):
  - Why is this case a dilemma?
  - Who are the key players?

  – What are the main issues/problems?
  – What, if anything, should be done to resolve the situation?
  – What are the consequences of each solution?
  – What would you do if you were the decision maker?
  – What did you learn from the case?
- Individuals in a discussion group may decide to carry out classroom research related to the case and then compare their results.

However, the case analysis is not complete, as a decision needs to be reached about the outcome of the case. This involves choosing one outcome from a variety of alternatives and saying why other outcomes are rejected.

Implementing case analysis

Before considering how cases can be prepared, it is necessary to consider the ways in which they might be used. If cases are to be used as a teacher-development activity within a school or institution, they can serve several useful functions, such as being made available as resources in support of a particular course or to address a particular issue. They can then be consulted by teachers as needed. For example, a group of case reports could be produced by first-year teachers, describing issues or problems they experience. These can be circulated and commented on by more experienced teachers. Or teachers teaching a particular course (e.g., advanced writing) could compile case reports dealing with different aspects of teaching advanced writing. These then form a resource file that future teachers of the course can consult. They can provide the focus of a discussion group that meets regularly to share and discuss reports.

Case studies can also serve as the basis for a dialogue between two teachers engaged in peer coaching and journal writing. Case examples can also be a component of a teaching portfolio.

Summary

Teachers have a great deal of accumulated expertise and knowledge, though much of this is often not available as a source of learning and reflection for others. By documenting examples of successful practice and exploring and writing about problematic issues that arise in teaching, a rich set of records can be produced that can be used as a basis for professional development. Cases can serve as a documentation of good practice, providing a valuable resource for novice teachers to explore the thinking and practices of experienced teachers. Through reading and commenting on cases, teachers can learn from the experience of others as well as develop a deeper understanding of their own beliefs and practices. Because cases are relatively easy to develop, they can serve as an initial teacher development activity, one that can be followed up by other more demanding activities, such as action research.

Example of a case study

The following is an example of a case study by a teacher in Hong Kong who was having problems encouraging her students to read (Tibbits, 1998, pp. 385–390).

Context

The school is a Chinese-medium primary school in Hong Kong. Classes are streamed on the results of success in mathematics and science, with the best students taking science. The science students are also best in English language. The arts students, however, have lower ability in science and are not motivated to study English language to the point that many of them give up altogether with English. Extensive reading is not actively encouraged in the school and attempts to persuade the students to read outside class are futile. Each class (from Forms 1 to 4) is given a set text as part of the English syllabus, and teachers often tell students they should read to improve their English. The texts for the class reader are the same for every class in the form.

Problem

The Form 4 class, which had a reputation for poor discipline, lack of motivation, and low English ability, had a set text (a simplified version of Roald Dahl's short stories) that was too difficult for them to understand (it was even difficult for the top science class to understand). Requests to change the set text were met with refusal on grounds that the students had already bought the text and parents would query the rationale for having different texts.

Solution

In order to increase the students' level of self-esteem and confidence regarding reading, the teacher decided to dispense quietly with the set text and encourage extensive reading for pleasure. Although the teacher considered using the library because it had simplified texts, she decided against this because it was difficult to get the students to go to the library in the first place and the library was not user-friendly—it was open only after school for 30 minutes, and at recess the students were not allowed to borrow books. So the teacher decided to establish a class library and introduce nonthreatening, uninterrupted sustained silent reading (USSR). However, the teacher was still faced with the problem of which texts to read. The school refused to buy more books because it already had a library. Another idea she had was to get the students to buy one book and exchange it with other students. However, she was concerned that the parents would complain about this too. The teacher then decided to look at what the publishers provide in the form of desk copies and donations at seminars. She went to various seminars and conferences in the following weeks and acquired a large number of readers (140) from the bags of goodies that publishers usually provide at seminars and conferences. She then organized a class library and assigned one class period per cycle to the activity. Students, in groups of eight, chose a text from one of four boxes of books in the class. The texts were arranged as follows: easy, not too hard, harder (for when you have time), hard (but interesting). When the choice was made, and the names noted, the students read quietly at their desks. The activity was a great success. After a few weeks, the reluctant readers approached the teacher to ask her if she would allow them to change the book at lunchtime so that they could read more.

Insights

According to the teacher, the success of the extensive reading program resulted from the following:

- *Freedom of choice.* The students could decide what to read and what level they wanted to read at.
- *Freedom of nonreading tasks.* The students did not have to account for the reading by writing a book report. They did not have to inform the teacher that they had read the book as she had appointed a class librarian (a student) to take care of all this.
- *Freedom to reject.* The students did not have to finish a book, and could change books whenever they desired.

- *Open discussion of books.* The teacher read the books herself, thus setting an example. When a student returned a book, the teacher then could ask him or her a question on the book in natural terms, such as what he or she thought of a particular character or turn of events.
- *Intrinsic motivation.* By giving students their choice of which books to read, by giving them books that were of potential interest to them, and by not insisting on an extrinsic account or report or test, the motivation to read was placed within each student's own responsibility.

References and further reading

Burns, A., & De Silva Joyce, H. (Eds.). (2000). *Teachers' voices 5: A new look at reading practices.* Sydney: National Centre for English Language Teaching and Research (NCELTR), Macquarie University.

Carnegie Task Force on Teaching as a Profession. (1986).

Carter, K., & Unklesbay, R. (1989). Cases in teaching and law. *Journal of Curriculum Studies* 21, pp. 527–536.

Farrell, T. S. C. (1998). Communicating with colleagues of a different culture. In J. C. Richards (Ed.), *Teaching in action* (pp. 125–128). Alexandria, VA: TESOL.

Geiger, J., & Shugarman, S. (1988). Portfolios and case studies to evaluate teacher education students and programs. *Action in Teacher Education* 10(3), pp. 31–34.

Jackson, J. (1997). Cases in TESOL teacher education: Creating a forum for reflection. *TESL Canada Journal* 14(2), pp. 1–16.

Johnson, K. E., & Golombek, P. (2002). *Teachers' narrative inquiry as professional development.* New York: Cambridge University Press.

Kagan, D. (1993). Contexts for the use of classroom cases. *American Educational Research Journal* 30(4), pp. 703–723.

Lynn, L. E. (1999). *Teaching and learning with cases: A guidebook.* New York: Chatham House Publishers.

Meijer, P. C., Verloop, N., & Beijaard, D. (1999). Exploring language teachers' practical knowledge about teaching reading comprehension. *Teaching and Teacher Education* 15, pp. 59–84.

Miller, B., & Kantrov, I. (1998). *A guide to facilitating cases in education.* Portsmouth, NH: Heinemann.

Olshtain, E., & Kupferberg, I. (1998). Reflective-narrative discourse of FL teachers exhibits professional knowledge. *Language Teaching Research (London)* 2(3), pp. 185–202.

Richards, J. C. (Ed.). (1998). *Teaching in action.* Alexandria, VA: TESOL.

Shulman, J. (Ed.). (1992). *Case methods in teacher education*. New York: Teachers College Press.

Shulman, L. (1992). Toward a pedagogy of cases. In J. Shulman (Ed.), *Case methods in teacher education* (pp. 1–30). New York: Teachers College Press.

Tibbits, J. (1998). Encouraging extensive reading in a secondary. In J. C. Richards (Ed.), *Teaching in action* (pp. 385–390). Alexandria, VA: TESOL.

Wassermann, S. (1993). *Getting down to cases: Learning to teach with case studies*. New York: Teachers College Press.

10 *Peer coaching*

The nature of peer coaching

Peer coaching is a procedure in which two teachers collaborate to help one or both teachers improve some aspect of their teaching. Robbins (1991, p. 1) defines peer coaching as follows:

A confidential process through which two or more professional colleagues work together to reflect on current practices, expand, refine, and build new skills, share ideas; teach one another; conduct classroom research; or solve problems in the workplace.

In peer coaching, a teacher and a colleague plan a series of opportunities to explore the teacher's teaching collaboratively. One adopts the role of coach or "critical friend" (someone in whom one has trust and confidence and who can offer constructive feedback in a positive and supportive manner) as some aspect of teaching or of classroom life is explored. During and after the process, the coach provides feedback and suggestions to the other teacher. The type of feedback the coach provides will depend on the goals that have been established. We prefer feedback to be nonjudgmental and nonevaluative in most cases. The coach offers observations and suggestions, but the other teacher makes his or her own decisions about what, if anything, to change as a result of the peer-coaching relationship. In other words, each teacher still has the main responsibility for his or her professional development and does not hand over control to a colleague. There may, however, be situations in which more direct input and evaluative feedback is required, such as when a novice teacher has been receiving very poor teaching evaluations or is experiencing difficulty with a teaching assignment and asks to work with a more experienced teacher to help address the problem.

Peer coaching can take the following forms:

- It can be a series of informal conversations between a teacher and a colleague about teaching, focusing on what is happening in the teacher's classrooms, what problems occur, and how these can be addressed.

- It can be collaboration between two teachers on the preparation of teaching materials (see vignette).
- A teacher and a coach can observe each other's lessons.
- Two teachers can co-teach lessons and observe each other's approach and teaching style.
- A teacher can videotape some of his or her lessons and later watch them together with the coach.

The following vignette is an example of a teacher who used peer coaching in Malaysia in order to develop and implement materials for an integrated EAP skills class – reading, writing, and listening. In this vignette he outlines how he used peer coaching to develop and implement new reading materials.

Vignette

Together with the curriculum coordinator (who actually proposed peer coaching at a meeting), I and one other teacher first wrote materials for an integrated skills module consisting of a reading and a writing section. For the reading section I was in charge of developing certain materials that focused on helping students to develop their skills in reading academic topics. When I finished this, we had the problem of how to implement the materials. So, as a peer coach I helped the other teacher by offering suggestions for using the materials in her classes while she was teaching. Sometimes I demonstrated how I would use the materials, and she also came to my classes and saw how I used the materials with my students. We found the whole peer-coaching relationship to be very helpful in making optimal use of the new materials in all our classes because we wanted to ensure uniform implementation of the new materials in all the classes. Both of us had the same ideas about implementation so we entered into other peer-coaching relationships with all the other teachers who were involved with these modules.

Mark Wilkinson

Reflection

- What made this peer relationship work for Mark and the other teacher?
- Why was the peer relationship that Mark experienced useful to the program?

Purpose, benefits, and types of peer coaching

Peer coaching is a developmental process (Joyce & Showers, 1982) and is an effective way to promote professional development. It provides opportunities for two teachers to look at teaching problems and to develop possible solutions. For example, peer coaching could be an opportunity for experienced teachers to work together to understand and implement a new curriculum. Or it could be used to help teachers new to an institution learn from more experienced colleagues because it provides a supportive context in which novice teachers can try out new teaching materials and approaches. It also helps develop collegiality between colleagues.

We have found that peer coaching offers benefits to the coach, the teacher, and the school. The coach has the satisfaction of helping another colleague and at the same time can revitalize his or her own teaching through the coaching process. Being asked to be a coach is also a sign of professional recognition. The collaborating teacher benefits in the peer-coaching relationship by gaining knowledge from a trusted peer, by getting constructive, nonthreatening feedback on his or her teaching, and by expanding his or her teaching repertoires. Peer coaching also reduces the sense of isolation that teachers tend to feel (Benedetti, 1997). The school benefits by strengthening the skills and collegiality of its teachers and by providing for training on the job, thus cutting down on the need for in-service training.

Types of peer coaching

There are three different types of peer coaching (Benedetti, 1997, p. 41): technical coaching, collegial coaching, and challenge coaching.

TECHNICAL COACHING

Technical coaching refers to a situation in which a teacher wants to learn a new teaching method or technique and seeks the assistance of another teacher who is experienced and more knowledgeable in this area. For example, a teacher might want to try teaching composition classes in an e-learning, distance mode with students in different parts of the campus. To learn more about it, the teacher seeks the advice of a colleague on how to implement this approach and the colleague advises him or her on the process, giving feedback as it is tried out. The following vignette outlines how a teacher wanted to share a method of teaching ESL writing using electronic mail with her colleagues.

Vignette

Over the years, I noticed that my students were reluctant to hand in printed essays because they perceived that these essays would be marked all in red and returned with a grade in the top corner. The students usually said that this was not helpful for them to improve their writing, so when I was at an international conference recently, I went to a workshop about using e-mail to help EFL students develop their writing. Because I am not a native English speaker, I always thought (and have been told) that e-mail was bad for our students' writing development because it encouraged bad writing habits. You can imagine my delight when I had finished this workshop on how to set up this system so that students could be encouraged to explore topics, write drafts, and get instant (well, near instant) feedback on their writing before they produced their final draft. Also, I discovered that we could set this system up where many students could interact with me and with each other to develop their writing, providing they followed some basic guidelines. When I returned to Japan, I was so excited about this system that I got permission from the head of the English Department to give a demonstration of how this would work. We all gathered in the computer room and we all had one computer so I actually took all my peers through the process of writing a real composition in English. Then I showed them a recording of how this system actually worked with my students. I was, of course, shy to perform this in front of my peers, but their wonderful response gave me the courage to help them further implement it in their classes. We all think it was a great success.

Yoko Nakamoto

Reflection

- What other ways do you think Yoko could have demonstrated her expertise to her colleagues?
- What expertise do you have that you could teach to your peers?

COLLEGIAL COACHING

Collegial coaching involves two teachers focusing on refining their existing teaching practices. In this situation, two teachers (one of them may have more knowledge of the teaching method than the other, and so would take a coaching role) may simply want to confirm their views on teaching. To do this, a teacher invites a colleague into his or her classroom to observe the class and offer constructive feedback as a critical friend (see example near the end of this chapter).

Vignette

I had been teaching listening comprehension for a long time and I wondered if I was still doing it the best way so I decided to ask a colleague who was also teaching listening comprehension at the school to come observe me. I really wanted to confirm to myself that I was still on the right track and I knew that this colleague had just recently finished her M.A. in TESOL degree so she would be well up in her current knowledge of theory and practice. Also, I had a good working relationship with her since she joined our school. Specifically, I had wanted to make sure that I was teaching my students useful strategies for taking notes from a recorded lecture. My colleague said that she had experience with this activity in her previous positions as an English teacher when she was studying in her M.A. TESOL course. I wanted to make sure my students understood that although learners may use different strategies to take notes, they must be able to use the notes to recall information. My colleague observed me teaching such a series of listening classes, and after each class we discussed the notes she had taken during the observation. I was delighted to learn from her that I was doing a pretty good job, and when we compared my intentions with what she thought I was seeking to achieve and what she thought the learners had learned, there was a pretty close match.

Eric Harmsen

Reflection

- What do you think are the main benefits of this type of collegial coaching?
- What other ways could they have gone about this approach to coaching?

CHALLENGE COACHING

Challenge coaching involves two teachers focusing on a problem that has arisen in some aspect of teaching, and they work jointly to resolve the problem. For example, a teacher you know may realize that he or she has a problem "getting through" to some of the students in a class and so invites a trusted peer to come observe the class in order to help identify the cause of the problem, and hopefully a solution.

Vignette
In our EAP program in Hong Kong a young American teacher (a U.S. teaching fellow) with little teaching experience was having trouble with some of his teaching assignments. I agreed to observe some of his classes and give him feedback and suggestions after each class. I also invited him to observe some of my classes and do the same. Through this process we began to explore alternative ways of approaching the materials, my junior colleague began to be able to see how he could adjust his own teaching strategies, and he gradually became much more confident. We also ended up becoming good friends.

Dino Mahoney

Reflection

- Do you think a peer coach should intervene in a class while observing? Why or why not?
- What are some ways in which a peer coach can give feedback following observation of a colleague's class?

Roles within peer coaching

Within the peer-coaching process, each member of the partnership has a specific role to play.

COACH

We like to think of the peer coach as a type of critical friend, another teacher who can observe and talk about teaching as part of a process of collaboration. This "friend" can provide a new lens to refocus and get a clearer understanding of teaching. Critical friendship as a means of teacher development was first discussed by Stenhouse (1975). He recommended that a teacher work with another person who could give advice as a friend rather than as a consultant in order to develop the reflective abilities of the teacher. However, it is important to remember that the word *critical* does not connote negativity as it does in everyday conversation; rather, it is used in its original Greek meaning, "to separate" and "to discern": to separate teaching into its parts and to discern how its parts work together (if they do) and how teaching is related to other areas of life. As we use the term, critical friends are teachers who collaborate with other teachers in order to encourage discussion and reflection that will improve the quality of teaching and learning (Farrell, 2001). A critical friend can thus provide another lens through which a teacher can obtain a clearer vision of his or her teaching, ask questions and provide classroom data as examined through a different lens, offer a critique and provide feedback in a nonjudgmental manner, and offer a trusting relationship in which conflict is seen as constructive by offering a different perspective on the classroom.

Gottesman (2000, p. 8) recommends that feedback be influenced by the motto for peer coaching: "No Praise, No Blame." This peer-coaching model is nonjudgmental, and evaluation is withheld until the relationship reaches a position where the teacher is ready, open, and willing to ask for suggestions for improvement. Gottesman (2000, p. 8) suggests that feedback statements from the peer coach be "specific in nature, about items the teacher can control, solicited rather than imposed, descriptive rather than evaluative, tactful, well timed, checked for clarity and simplicity, dealing with behaviors rather than personalities (of either teacher or students), not personality-driven, and well organized." Thus, the coach should be an active listener so that the peer can find his or her own solutions to whatever issue is being discussed. The following vignette is an example of technical coaching. Lyn, an experienced reading teacher in an EAP program in Singapore, had just taken over the reading program in the school and noticed that the program did not have any rate-building classes in the courses.

Vignette

I wanted to get all the reading teachers to use this method because ongoing rate-building exercises are necessary and very helpful to improve the students' overall reading skill. I didn't have the time to coach all ten teachers, so I decided to coach one other teacher, the most senior teacher in terms of teaching experience, who in turn would coach the other teachers. Both of us agreed on times and classes where I could coach the other teacher on handling a rate-building session in a reading class. I went over the following points with the other teacher and looked for their implementation when I observed the teacher's classes:

- Make sure students understand the purpose of the exercise – not to get a head start reading before the clock; read for gist, not 100% comprehension; not to look back at reading when answering comprehension questions, and so on.
- Let students know a target reading rate they should work toward – what's appropriate for different kinds of reading materials.

- Students record rate and percentage on reading chart, take notes on vocabulary they want to review.

The teacher seemed to have covered all and I was happy that she would be able to coach some of the other teachers. This has worked out well for everyone in the program.

Lyn May

Reflection

- Do you think peer coaching is an efficient way to implement changes in the curriculum? Why? Why not?
- What other methods could Lyn have adopted to coach the teachers?

TEACHER

The collaborating teacher needs to be willing to cooperate with the coach and critical friend, remain open-minded, and be interested in learning about new ways to approach teaching. A teacher who is willing to try to improve his or her teaching is not admitting weakness, but rather is simply trying to find better ways to teach his or her students (Gottesman, 2000).

Gottesman (2000, p. 37) suggests the following roles for a teacher in a peer-coaching relationship:

- Be committed to peer coaching as a way of analyzing and improving instruction.
- Be willing to develop and use a common language of collaboration in order to discuss the total teaching act without praise or blame.
- Be willing to enter into a peer-coaching relationship (e.g., by requesting a classroom observation visit and by observing as a coach if asked).
- Be open-minded and willing to look for better ways of conducting classroom business.
- Act as a colleague and as a professional.

Procedures used for peer coaching

Peer coaching can be conducted on a formal or an informal level. At an informal level, a teacher and a colleague can simply sit down and discuss his or her teaching in the form of conversations about what happened in the teacher's classroom. The two teachers might also undertake a curriculum development project together, jointly developing materials for a course and discussing the thinking behind the materials. If two teachers are teaching the same subject area, they can analyze what they are doing and make suggestions for improving the curriculum or materials. Two teachers can also co-teach lessons and observe each other's approach and teaching style. They can also videotape lessons and watch the tapes together. The coach can also act as an expert in a particular area and help the colleague develop the knowledge or skills needed to teach the subject.

Three initial phases are often useful in implementing peer coaching: *peer watching, peer feedback,* and *peer coaching* (Gottesman, 2000).

- *Peer watching*. The first phase, peer watching, involves a teacher observing another teacher teach but without making any comments or giving any suggestions after the class. The teacher can take notes but should not talk or comment to his or her colleague about the class during this phase. It is important to remember that peer watching is just that, watching and not interfering in any way during the lesson or sharing the results with the teacher after the lesson. For example, a teacher might invite a peer to watch him or her teach a class on reading comprehension. The teacher is interested in knowing more about how he or she gives instructions during class, so he or she asks a peer to observe the class and to focus on how instructions are given throughout the lesson. The teacher gets used to having an observer in the class and the peer gets practice in taking notes while observing a class. However, the peer does not discuss his or her observations at this stage. When both teachers feel comfortable with the process, they can move on to the next stage, peer feedback.
- *Peer feedback*. This next short phase is a transition between watching and coaching. During peer feedback, the coach, who has collected data, presents this information to his or her peer. No coaching or suggestions for improvement take place in this phase, just a presentation of the facts. The peer can develop his or her note-taking skills during this phase and can try out different data-gathering devices such as checklists or video- and audio-recording.
- *Peer coaching*. This crucial last phase in the process is where real coaching takes place. It is where the coach plans and offers suggestions for improvement if the teacher has asked for this type of direct input.

Peer coaching and mentoring

Mentoring is a particular form of peer coaching. It is a process whereby an experienced teacher works with a novice teacher, giving guidance and feedback. Mentor teachers often receive special training and support for their role as mentor. They have usually been drawn from veteran teachers within a school who help beginners learn the philosophy, cultural values, and established sets of behaviors expected by the school employing them (Little, 1990).

For language teachers new to a school, Malderez and Bodoczky (1999, p. 4) describe some different roles that mentors can play and suggest that most mentors will be involved "to a greater or lesser degree in all five roles."

- They can be models who inspire and demonstrate.
- They can be acculturators who show new teachers the ropes.
- They can be sponsors who introduce the new teachers to the "right people."
- They can be supporters who are there to listen and to encourage new teachers who may need to let off steam.
- They can be educators who act as sounding boards for the articulation of ideas to help new teachers achieve professional learning objectives.

Peer coaching is generally different from a mentor-protégé relationship in that the responsibilities are more restricted and the relationship between the coach and the teacher is more equal. The purpose of peer coaching is to build collegiality as teachers develop themselves professionally.

Implementing peer coaching

Peer coaching may be implemented in the following ways:

- *Find out teachers' views on peer coaching.* Initially it is important to provide those interested in peer coaching with information about what peer coaching is (and is not) and to give them a chance to discuss any concerns or misgivings. At this stage, teachers can discuss how peer coaching might be able to help them with their development as teachers. Questions that might be discussed include the following:
  - What does peer coaching involve and how can it help you in your professional development?
  - Do you think peer coaching as professional development takes your needs into account?
  - Do you think there will be any problems in observing lessons (or in being observed)?

- Do you think there will be any problems giving feedback?
- What do you hope you will achieve by taking part in peer coaching?
- In what areas would you be willing to serve as an "expert" coach?
- *Provide structure for teachers.* It is necessary to provide structure and incentives during the early stages of peer coaching. This structure can be in the form of providing time in the schedule so that peer coaching can occur. It is also important to establish incentives for the teachers to engage in peer coaching. Giving teachers time off to engage in peer coaching as part of their professional development will go a long way to achieving this. The administration can further help the peer-coaching process to take hold by finding coverage for a class that the teachers are supposed to teach at the time of the peer coaching, having the principal cover some classes, and/or using in-service days for peer-coaching activities.
- *Select the form of peer-coaching activity (e.g., observation, materials writing).* Teams can now decide what they will focus their peer-coaching activity on. One of the most common forms of peer coaching is where peers watch each other teach classes in order to reflect on their current practices. Teachers might also want to expand, refine, and/or build new teaching skills by watching each other teach. Alternatively, one peer might want to teach another peer a specific method or technique of teaching while getting feedback on this new technique at the same time. Another form of peer coaching could be watching videos of specific teaching techniques and critiquing these techniques while trying to implement them in their own classes. Discussions can focus on the appropriateness of these techniques and how they could be (and were) adapted in their own classes. This would combine video watching and classroom observations.
- *Plan how and when to carry out the activity.* Peer coaching works best when teachers build trust with each other, set their own schedules, and engage in peer coaching on a regular basis. For real peer coaching to take place, it has to be performed on a system of request: One teacher requests a peer to coach him or her on some aspect of teaching in order to improve his or her teaching. There is no reporting to administrators, no "expert" or "clite" team, and no fixed administrative schedule.
- *Choose specific topics.* The teacher chooses a peer coach and requests a visit or chooses the topic for collaboration with the coach. The teacher's responsibility is to be as specific as possible about what he or she wants the peer to coach him or her on. For example, if the collaboration

involves a classroom visit, the teacher may want to focus on such topics as wait time, patterns of classroom interaction (teacher-to-students and student-to-student), the clarity, type, and mode of delivery of instructions, the teacher's use of praise, and the type and frequency of teacher's questions, to name but a few. If the peer-coaching collaboration is focused on classroom research, and the publication of this research in a teacher's magazine or academic journal, then the teacher can seek a peer who has experience in publishing and work with the coach to publish a paper in a selected journal. In this way, the coach will know exactly what is expected from him or her.

- *Reflect and review.* In any peer-coaching process it is important for both the teacher and the coach to step back from the relationship in order to reflect on what happened. This review is vital for the future of the peer relationship. Any analysis of the peer-coaching process should seek answers to the following questions:
  - Was the feedback specific and only related to the topic requested by the teacher?
  - What kind of language was used in the feedback session? Was it judgmental and/or evaluative? If so, how can this be avoided in the future?
  - Will the peer-coaching process be helpful for the teacher? For example, if it involved classroom observations, will this lead to more effective teaching?
  - Will the teacher seek another classroom visit?
  - Is the teacher willing to act as a coach now?

Teachers entering a peer-coaching relationship should be aware of problems that might occur for both the teacher and the peer coach. Time is an often-cited problem. The demands of time need to be considered. The coach needs time to discuss and observe the teacher and the teacher needs time to learn from the coach. We have found that if the peer coaching is a formal activity sanctioned by the school, then the coach must be allowed time-release from teaching so that he or she can combine coaching with teaching. The teacher also needs time and opportunity to analyze his or her own teaching and to be able to articulate these to the coach. Coaching can be demanding if coaches are not clear about their exact roles in the peer-coaching relationship. For this they need to be trained somewhat in the basic skills of mentoring and coaching. Additionally, peer-coaching relationships can sometimes be unpredictable. This can be especially true if both the teacher and the coach feel unclear about their roles and responsibilities.

Also, for the relationship to be effective, a culture of trust must be built up in the school and in the relationship.

Summary

Peer coaching is a form of teacher collaboration in which one teacher coaches a peer in performing a teaching activity. This form of collaboration offers benefits to all the participants. Peer coaching can take the form of technical coaching, collegial coaching, or challenge coaching. It is important to clearly define the roles of both the coach and teacher from the very beginning of the process so that a culture of trust can be established as early as possible in the collaboration. When institutions want to implement peer coaching, the teachers should be consulted about their concerns and informed about their roles in the process and the type of structure the institution will provide. Sufficient time must be allowed both by the teachers involved in the peer coaching and by the institution in which the peer coaching occurs.

Example of peer coaching

The following is a summary of a peer-coaching situation in Japan (Sagliano, Sagliano, & Stewart, 1998).

Context

The context is an English-medium 4-year university in Japan with a liberal arts program. A unique feature of the program is that some courses are taught by interdisciplinary pairs of teachers. The program's philosophy is that this interdisciplinary (language-content) exchange can promote critical reflection on teaching.

Participants

The participants in this study were three interdisciplinary teams of teachers. There were three ESOL faculty members who had all taught Japanese university students for a number of years. Their discipline-area teaching partners (two in history and one in religion) had many combined years of higher education teaching experience; one had a newly minted Ph.D. All

participants were committed to developing courses and teaching collaboratively across disciplines.

Process (peer coaching)

Peer coaching is a natural extension of team teaching. The process of peer
coaching in the three cases grew out of team-teaching experiences. In all
cases, the desire for peer coaching came from a perceived need in all three
teams to better integrate language and content instruction. In one case, the
co-teachers began their course with a high level of mutual trust. In the others,
that trust had to be earned over time. As the teams worked out their course
learning objectives, developed materials, and instructed together, they were
critically appraising each other's work. In short, they met regularly to work
on specific aspects of their course and their development as teachers.

Outcomes

Each of the three cases generated different outcomes. One teaching pair
discovered through peer coaching the value of open, ongoing dialogue for
clarifying viewpoints about students and tasks. Too much of what teachers
believe they know is unstated and assumed to be shared knowledge. Another
teaching team found that their willingness and capacity to listen carefully to
each other's points of view grew, while reacting to student feedback resulted
in more innovative teaching styles for both of them. In the third case, an
ESOL teacher advised a historian on the appropriateness of subject content
for Japanese college students. This helped to sensitize the instructor to the
importance of developing appropriate ways for introducing new material to
students.

Insights

Several insights were gained from this peer-coaching example. First, teachers may be reluctant to change instructional habits owing to the nature of the
organizational structure of colleges, the teaching profession itself, and the
inherent preferences of teachers. Thus, energetic leadership and support by
administrators are vital to the successful promotion of peer coaching. Second, teachers may have conflicting values. Again, these sources of conflict
should be worked out with administrative support. Third, teachers may be
uneasy about coaching each other. This requires the cultivation of trust and
sensitivity, combined with the ability to be candid yet considerate. Fourth,
teachers may balk at spending time to develop peer-coaching relationships.

Peer-coaching relationships can quickly come to be seen as unwanted additional work. Once teachers agree to work collaboratively to improve instruction, it is vital to the success of the venture that the goals, tasks, and responsibilities of the partners are clearly understood at all times.

References and further reading

Bailey, K., Dale, T., & Squire, B. (1992). Some reflections on collaborative language teaching. In D. Nunan (Ed.), *Collaborative language learning and teaching* (pp. 162–178). New York: Cambridge University Press.

Benedetti, T. (1997). Enhancing teaching and teacher education with peer coaching. *TESOL Journal* 7(1), pp. 41–42.

Bova, B. M., & Philips, R. E. (1981). *The mentor relationship: A study of mentors and protégés in business and academia.* ED 208 233.

Farrell, T. S. C. (2001). Critical friendships: Colleagues helping each other develop. *English Language Teaching Journal* 55(4), pp. 368–374.

Glatthorn, A. (1987). Cooperative professional development: Peer-centered options for teacher growth. *Educational Leadership* 45, pp. 31–35.

Gottesman, B. (2000). *Peer coaching for educators.* 2d ed. London: Scarecrow Press.

Joyce, B., & Showers, B. (1982). The coaching of teaching. *Educational Leadership* 40(1), pp. 4–10.

Kaufman, D. (1997). Collaborative approaches in preparing teachers for content-based and language-enhanced settings. In M. A. Snow & D. M. Brinton (Eds.), *The content-based classroom: Perspectives on integrating language and content* (pp. 175–186). New York: Longman.

Kaufman, D., & Brooks, J. G. (1996). Interdisciplinary collaboration in teacher education: A constructivist approach. *TESOL Quarterly* 30, pp. 231–251.

Kullman, J. (1998). Mentoring and the development of reflective practice: Concepts and context. *System* 26, pp. 471–484.

Little, J. W. (1990). The mentor phenomenon and the social organization of teaching. In C. B. Courtney (Ed.), *Review of research in education* 16 (pp. 297–325). Washington, DC: American Educational Research Association.

Malderez, A., & Bodoczky, C. (1999). *Mentor courses: A resource book for trainer-trainers.* Cambridge: Cambridge University Press.

McCowen, M., Ewell, B., & McConnell, P. (1995). Creative conversations: An experiment in interdisciplinary team teaching. *College Teaching* 43, pp. 127–131.

Robbins, P. (1991). How to plan and implement a peer coaching pro-
    gramme. Alexandria, VA: Association for Supervision Curriculum
    Development.
Sagliano, J., Sagliano, M., & Stewart, T. (1998). Peer coaching through team
    teaching: Three cases of teacher development. *Asia-Pacific Journal of
    Teacher Education and Development* 1(1), pp. 73–82.
Stenhouse, L. (1975). *An introduction to curriculum research and develop-
    ment*. London: Heinemann.

11 *Team teaching*

The nature of team teaching

Team teaching (sometimes called pair teaching) is a process in which two or more teachers share the responsibility for teaching a class. The teachers share responsibility for planning the class or course, for teaching it, and for any follow-up work associated with the class such as evaluation and assessment. It thus involves a cycle of team planning, team teaching, and team follow-up. It allows teachers to cooperate as equals, although when teachers with differing levels of experience share the same class, some elements of a coaching relationship may also occur. We should point out that we do not regard shared teaching as all that team teaching involves. Teachers have sometimes reported to us that by team teaching they mean two teachers planning independently the different parts of a lesson, and while one is teaching the other uses the opportunity to mark homework or take a break! This is not team teaching but simply team planning. The following is an example of two teachers sharing an EFL class in Japan.

Vignette

A Japanese colleague and I often team-teach some of our classes. We feel that it's a good way for students to experience a different kind of lesson and we both learn from watching how the other teaches the class. We always plan well ahead to make sure we complement each other during the lesson. Sometimes I do the lead in part of an activity and my colleague takes over from me. If there is a group-work activity, of course we are both involved in moving around and facilitating the task. Because I am a native speaker, my colleague sometimes likes me to do the part of an activity that he is not so confident about – such as reading out a dialogue or reading out a section from a reading passage. But I feel she is much better than me at

159

handling other parts of the lesson, such as taking the students through a grammar activity.

Charles Guyotte

Reflection

- How do you think two teachers should decide which parts of the lesson they will teach?
- How do you think students benefit from having two teachers teach a lesson?

Purpose and benefits of team teaching

In team teaching, both teachers generally take equal responsibility for the different stages of the teaching process. The shared planning, decision making, teaching, and review that result serve as a powerful medium of collaborative learning. Although the logistics of implementing team teaching can be difficult, there are many benefits to taking part in it on a regular basis.

- *Collegiality.* An important benefit of team teaching is that it promotes collegiality among teachers in a school. An unfortunate fact of school life is that teachers are often unaware of the strengths and expertise of their colleagues. Teachers have often reported to us that team teaching enables them to learn a great deal about each other and develop a closer professional and personal relationship.
- *Different roles.* When colleagues share a class, each has an opportunity to move between teaching and observing or assisting, providing a change from the pace and demands of a solo-taught class. The second teacher can also help out in ways that would be impossible for a single teacher to manage (e.g., monitoring pair or group work).
- *Combined expertise.* When two teachers teach a class, they can learn from each other's strengths when planning and teaching lessons. Each teacher will have different ideas on how to deal with any difficulties in the lesson, as well as a different body of experience to draw on. Their combined degrees of knowledge and expertise are bound to lead to a stronger lesson plan. This gives each team member a new perspective on teaching and learning. Both come to recognize and appreciate that alternative methods and techniques of teaching and evaluating lessons exist. According to Shannon and Meath-Lang (1992, p. 131), successful

team teachers "recognized the gifts, skills and expertise of the partner without feeling denigrated, or in any way less skillful." During the lesson itself, the extra set of eyes can be useful when a student misunderstands something. The person who is teaching at that moment can carry on with the lesson, while the other teacher can deal with the student's problem.

- *Teacher-development opportunities.* Team teaching is an effective means of teacher development. It provides a ready-made classroom observation situation, but without any evaluative component. As two teachers observe each other teach, they can contribute constructive comments and feedback. Team teaching also helps to develop creativity because when team teaching, both teachers know they are teaching for their colleague as well as for their learners.
- *Learner benefits.* Learners also benefit from having two teachers present in the class. They hear two different models of language, depending on where the teachers are from. They experience two different styles of teaching. There is also more opportunity for individual interaction with a teacher. Team teaching thus facilitates individualized instruction because it creates learning environments involving closer personal contact between teacher and learner.

For team teaching to be successful, we have found that it is important for both teachers to have a strong sense of confidence in each other. One survey of sixty language teachers who had experience with team teaching found that their greatest concern had to do with "trust and mutual respect" and that team teaching could only achieve its full potential if these were present (Bailey, Dale, & Squire, 1992). Team teaching should therefore be well coordinated so that students don't feel that the lesson is disjointed. It is also important for team members to be aware of each other's teaching style and to try to establish transitions between different styles. Team teaching with a colleague thus demonstrates the old saying "Two heads are better than one" if the teams are set up properly and each member knows and follows agreed-upon roles within the team.

Procedures used for team teaching

Decide on the roles within a team-teaching collaboration

The success of any team-teaching situation depends on the skills of the two teachers and how clearly they have understood their roles within the team. In planning for team teaching it is important to be aware of the different types of teaching arrangements there are so that the two teachers can choose or adapt those that best suit their situation. In our experience, a brown-bag lunch at the beginning of a term is a good way to introduce the idea of team teaching and the different ways it can be carried out and to let teachers who have tried it share their experiences with others.

The following are examples of different team-teaching collaborations:

- *Equal partners.* Two teachers see themselves as having an equal degree of experience and knowledge and key decisions are shared and achieved through discussion and negotiation. This relationship is typical when experienced teachers take part in team teaching. The two teachers are equally responsible for all stages of the lesson: planning, delivery, monitoring, and checking. The following vignette illustrates a situation in which new EFL teachers in a language institute found themselves at the same stage of inexperience and thus decided that team teaching might benefit both teachers equally.

Vignette

I recently started working for a private language institute. When I started, I realized that most of the other native-speaking teachers and I were in the same situation – we had relatively little teaching experience and were fairly uncertain as to what being an EFL teacher really involved. We decided to pair up and take time to team-teach one of our classes a week. We met before each class and worked out who would teach each part of the lesson. While one taught, the other observed. After the class, we met to review the lesson and to compare notes on what worked and what didn't. It was a very useful experience and everyone thought we developed confidence and improved our teaching as a consequence.

Rosemary Harding

Reflection

- What are some of the benefits that inexperienced teachers can get from team teaching?
- What might be some of the potential difficulties with novice teachers taking part in team teaching?

- *Leader and participant.* In this situation one teacher is given a leadership role in terms of making key decisions about the team-teaching experience. This may be appropriate when one teacher has a great deal of experience with team teaching and the other is new to it.

- *Mentor and apprentice.* In this situation one teacher is recognized as an expert teacher and the other is a novice. The mentor will typically hold a greater level of responsibility for decision making than the novice. This type of relationship is helpful when beginning teachers are being given support through team teaching.
- *Advanced speaker and less proficient speaker.* In some situations an advanced speaker of English (who may be a native speaker) may team-teach with a less proficient speaker. Typically, in these situations the advanced speaker takes responsibility for those aspects of the lesson that are more linguistically demanding.
- *Fluent, untrained native speaker and experienced nonnative speaker.* This situation is common in some countries where native speakers who have no EFL/ESL teacher training or experience are invited to team-teach with local and fully trained English language teachers who have the expertise and knowledge about teaching. Sometimes these untrained native speakers are called conversation partners and "speak" with the teacher and the students while the teacher has responsibility for organizing the lesson.

Delivering a team-taught lesson

A crucial factor in team teaching is determining the responsibilities of each teacher during a lesson. The different teacher roles, discussed in the preceding section, may lead to different responsibilities within the lesson. In some situations, both teachers have equal responsibilities within the lesson. However, this is not always the case, especially if one teacher is less proficient in English than the other or if there are power differentials between the teachers (e.g., mentor/apprentice, or leader/participant). Responsibilities will also change depending on if it is to be a one-shot lesson or a series of lessons. Depending on which type of collaboration both teachers have agreed upon, the lessons need to be jointly planned in advance and responsibilities assigned. The following vignette describes a teacher's evaluation of a team-teaching collaboration.

Vignette

My teaching partner and I were both amazed at how our two different contributions worked together. We both had similar teaching styles; planning together and conducting a class together was easier than we had expected; learners found it pleasurable and interesting seeing two instructors work well together – this was more like a culture shock to them because in their native countries teachers usually do not team-teach.

We both felt that team teaching was worth our efforts and was a means for professional development. Our goal was to engage learners in cooperative learning, and not to judge our teaching styles. What we learned by circulating around the class and through observation was that the learners enjoyed working together with each other. Far more interesting were students' positive comments about team teaching and the chance to interact with two instructors at the same time. All and all, we had fun working together and decided that we should engage in team teaching at least once a week, giving each other a chance to become both the protagonist and the observer. What did we both learn about the team-teaching process? It takes a lot more than simply planning a lesson for team teaching to be successful. Teachers must be prepared to accept their colleagues as equals, respect their teaching styles and expertise, and be ready to improvise because no plan has been written in stone and one never knows how the students will react to team teaching. Awareness of cultural differences is important because some learners might react unfavorably to a teaching method that they are not familiar with, and teachers must be prepared to face any negative responses without taking offense.

Angelique A. Schinas

Reflection

- What problems might arise when two teachers take equal responsibility for planning and teaching a class?
- What factors do you think are important in choosing a team-teaching partner?

Implementing team teaching

We have found the following factors to be most important when setting up team teaching and that these issues need to be carefully thought about to maintain teachers' interest and enthusiasm in team teaching over the long term.

Decide on the goals of the program

When setting up a team-teaching program it is important to decide what the purpose of team teaching is going to be. Is it to help new teachers with their teaching assignments, to help novice teachers develop their teaching skills, to establish a greater sense of collegiality within the institution, to create the role of mentors for senior teachers, or to simply give teachers a break from their usual teaching routines?

Prepare for team teaching

As with any innovation in teaching, team teaching will work best if teachers understand what it is, what its goals are, how it works, and what problems to anticipate. This can be achieved through planning and discussion among teachers, during which decisions can be made about the frequency of team teaching and the logistics of implementing it. Decisions can also be made about who will participate and the kind of support and preparation they need. This could take the form of a seminar in which teachers share their experience with team teaching or a workshop in which participants discuss how they would team-teach different kinds of lessons.

As with any innovation, before committing to a full-scale implementation of team teaching during a whole semester, it may be worthwhile to try it out first on a trial basis with one or two teams over one or two lessons, and discuss how successful it was and what problems it raises. Only later will a wider-scale version be implemented. This planning should include what activities and materials will be used in the lessons and who will take responsibility for the different stages in the lessons.

Address teachers' concerns

If you are a supervisor or program coordinator, it is important that each team know what the overall aims of the team-teaching program are and what the relationship of these aims to their own professional developments. Team teaching may not be for everyone and normally is more effective when teachers participate on a voluntary basis. The following teachers' concerns need to be anticipated:

- How much time will it take?
- Is this extra work or part of my normal schedule?
- Do I get to choose whom I will teach with?
- What happens if the teacher has a different teaching style from mine?
- What happens if we disagree over how a lesson should be taught?
- What happens if I end up taking all the responsibility and doing all the work?
- What do we do if the students like one teacher more than the other?
- Is evaluation involved?
- What's in it for me?

These concerns become especially important when the teams are made up of a less proficient and a more advanced speaker of the target language.

Decide model(s) of team teaching to be used and identify participants

The next step is to decide on a suitable approach to team teaching and the roles the participants will be expected to play. If teachers participate on a voluntary basis, the choice of partners will be important.

Monitor progress

After each class, teachers will want to discuss the success of the lesson, how the students reacted, and ways the lesson could be improved in the future. In order to ensure a positive team-teaching experience, it is also useful for all teachers engaged in team teaching to meet regularly to discuss any problems they are experiencing and to discuss ways of resolving them. The teachers can use these forums to discuss progress, suggest adjustments or changes, and voice any other concerns that have come up during the team-teaching sessions.

Evaluate what was learned

After trying out team teaching, it is important to find out what was learned from it and whether it is worth continuing. Views of students and participating teachers need to be sought.

- *Students*. The students in team-taught classes can be asked to comment on how they viewed the lessons in terms of their perceived interest, enjoyment, and what they thought they had learned. The impact of the students' motivation to learn English is important in judging the effectiveness of a team-teaching program. Questions such as the following could be asked:
  - Do you think your English has improved through team teaching? In what ways?
  - Are you more interested in learning English when your classes are taught this way?
  - How do these classes differ from other classes you have?
  - Would you like to continue studying English this way?

- *Teachers*. Teachers can be surveyed about their perceptions of the team-teaching process and what they liked or disliked about it. Questions such as the following could be asked:
  - What are the advantages of team teaching?
  - What are the disadvantages of team teaching?
  - How do you think it affects the students' language learning?
  - Do you think your students enjoyed this mode of teaching?
  - What suggestions would you like to make to improve the existing team-teaching program?
  - Would you like to continue with this way of teaching English?

Summary

Team teaching involves a shared and collaborative approach to planning, developing, teaching, and evaluating lessons. It is important that both members of the team take equal responsibility for each stage of this process. The shared planning, decision making, teaching, and review that result from the team-teaching process serve as a powerful medium of collaborative learning. Implementing successful team teaching requires that both teachers have a strong sense of confidence in each other. Team teaching should also be well coordinated and the lessons well monitored so that students have a sense that the lesson is not disjointed. After the lessons, the team should review the process in order to evaluate what was learned not only by the students but also by the teachers, so that all concerned can decide whether to continue with these lessons or not.

Example of team teaching

The following is a summary of a team-teaching situation in a university in Japan (Stewart, Sagliano, & Sagliano, 2002).

Context

The context is an English-medium 4-year university in Japan with a liberal arts program. The program incorporates a sheltered immersion approach using pairs of language and content teachers to lead classes. This program is institutionalized in the first 2 years, and students in it develop English proficiency as they learn content disciplines in the humanities and social sciences.

Participants

This interdisciplinary team-teaching situation has been implemented institution-wide. The makeup of the faculty is divided evenly between language and content disciplines. More than 80% of the faculty are foreign and all speak English.

Process

For newcomers, the process begins with an orientation to the college's mission and teaching philosophy. This includes workshops on ways to make interdisciplinary team teaching work. Teachers choose partners by making a ranked selection of desired co-teachers prior to each term. Administrators then set the teams by matching first and second choices. Some pairs must be assigned. Each teaching pair negotiates its own procedures for developing and teaching a course. Normally, the instructor of the academic discipline will suggest content for the course. Once appropriate learning objectives and content have been negotiated, teams set out to jointly create materials that meet both content and language objectives for the course. As equal partners, co-teachers jointly create materials, teach, and determine grades. Courses are self-contained, with instructors working simultaneously in the classroom. The instructional time is a collaborative effort. They trade off the lead and supporting teaching roles.

Outcomes

College policy has shaped how team teaching has evolved. Both instructors must be present in the classroom at all times. Furthermore, each instructor is guaranteed equal input into the computation of final course grades. Except for these obligations, the language and content partners are free to arrange the partnership in a mutually acceptable manner. Early on in this experiment, many teams were most comfortable with variations on the adjunct model of team teaching; that is, although they were in the same classroom together, they segregated their teaching time. Teaching "linked" components to the same course allowed instructors to exercise freedom in lesson planning, materials' design, and classroom instruction. As more experience and confidence were gained, some teaching teams began to adopt a more fully collaborative approach to interdisciplinary team teaching. They tried to blend instruction in language and content as seamlessly as possible.

Insights

Successful implementation of team teaching demands time, patience, honest reflection, reevaluation, and response by faculty and administrators. Every teacher should continuously be developing his or her pedagogy. Administrators should schedule time and channel activities into a program of continuous professional development. To be effective, institutions need to require participation and must provide incentives for involvement in regular workshops. Veteran team teachers should mentor newcomers and talk frankly about their experiences. Guidelines should be provided to team teachers to ensure that they are asking the right questions. Ideally, administrators should actively team-teach to better understand the commitments involved. Instructors need time to meet before and/or after lessons. Teachers also need appropriate spaces where they can hold meetings undisturbed.

References and further reading

Bailey, K., Dale, T., & Squire, B. (1992). Some reflections on collaborative language teaching. In D. Nunan (Ed.), *Collaborative language learning and teaching* (pp. 162–178). New York: Cambridge University Press.

Bailey, K. M., Curtis, A., & Nunan, D. (2001). Pursuing professional development: The self as source. Boston: Heinle & Heinle.

Boice, R. (1992). *The new faculty member: Supporting and fostering professional development*. San Francisco: Jossey-Bass.

Chamberlain, R. (1980). The SP of the E. In *Team teaching in ESP, ELT documents* 106 (pp. 97–108). London: British Council English Teaching Information Centre.

Dudley-Evans, T. (1983). An experiment in team-teaching of English for occupational purposes. In T. Dudley-Evans (Ed.), *Papers on team-teaching and syllabus design, Occasional papers* 27 (pp. 35–41). Singapore: SEAMEO Regional English Language Centre.

Dudley-Evans, T. (1984). The team-teaching of writing skills. In R. Williams, J. M. Swales, & J. Kirkman (Eds.), *Common ground: Shared interests in ESP and communication studies, ELT Documents* 117 (pp. 127–134). Oxford: Pergamon.

Hatton, E. J. (1985). Team teaching and teacher orientation to work: Implications for the preservice and inservice preparation of teachers. *Journal of Education for Teaching* 11(3), pp. 228–244.

Shannon, N. B., & Meath-Lang, B. (1992). Collaborative language teaching: A co-investigation. In D. Nunan (Ed.), *Collaborative language learning and teaching* (pp. 120–140). Cambridge: Cambridge University Press.

Struman, P. (1992). Team teaching: A case study from Japan. In D. Nunan (Ed.), *Collaborative language learning and teaching* (pp. 141–161). Cambridge: Cambridge University Press.

Stewart, T. (2001). Raising the status of ESP educators through integrated team teaching. *Asian Journal of English Language Teaching* 11, pp. 45–67.

Stewart, T., Sagliano, M., & Sagliano, J. (2002). Merging expertise: Promoting partnerships between language and content specialists. In J. Crandall & D. Kaufman (Eds.), *Content-based language instruction* (pp. 29–44). Alexandria, VA: TESOL.

Teemant, A., Bernhardt, E., & Rodríguez-Muñoz, M. (1997). Collaborating with content-area teachers: What we need to share. In M. A. Snow & D. M. Brinton (Eds.), *The content-based classroom: Perspectives on integrating language and content* (pp. 311–318). New York: Longman.

12 *Action research*

The nature of action research

Action research refers to teacher-conducted classroom research that seeks to clarify and resolve practical teaching issues and problems. The term "action research" refers to two dimensions of this kind of activity: The word *research* in "action research" refers to a systematic approach to carrying out investigations and collecting information that is designed to illuminate an issue or problem and to improve classroom practice. The word *action* refers to taking practical action to resolve classroom problems. Action research takes place in the teacher's own classroom and involves a cycle of activities centering on identifying a problem or issue, collecting information about the issue, devising a strategy to address the issue, trying out the strategy, and observing its effects. The nature of action research, however, with its cycle of observing, analyzing, acting, and reviewing, indicates that it is an activity that takes time to carry out and hence requires a considerable time commitment. For this reason, it is often more usefully viewed as a collaborative activity. The practical improvements action research seeks to bring about are not its only benefits, however. Through the process of planning and carrying out action research, teachers can develop a deeper understanding of many issues in teaching and learning as well as acquire useful classroom investigation skills.

Action research has the following characteristics:

- Its primary goal is to improve teaching and learning in schools and classrooms and it is conducted during the process of regular classroom teaching.
- It is usually small-scale and is intended to help resolve problems rather than simply be research for its own sake.
- It can be carried out by an individual teacher or in collaboration with other teachers.

The following vignette shows how a teacher makes use of action research.

171

Vignette

I have been interested for some time in the affective dimension of my classes and decided to carry out an action research project to explore this issue. My research was prompted by the fact that I felt my classes of teenage learners were sometimes becoming predictable and that students' attention seemed to be lagging. To address this issue I decided to investigate the effects of introducing a number of changes into my classes. These consisted of one or more of the following: (*a*) playing calm music at intervals during the lesson (a 2-minute "music break"); (*b*) stopping the lesson to play a short game, to break up the lesson; (*c*) playing a short Total Physical Response-type activity. After trying these strategies for a number of weeks, I asked the students to complete a questionnaire, telling me whether they enjoyed my classes more. I found that most students thought the lessons were now more interesting; a few thought they didn't make much difference, and no one objected to them. One thing I have learned from this is the importance of experimenting with different teaching and motivational strategies on a regular basis and asking students for their impressions of their usefulness.

Robert Dickey

Reflection

- What benefits do you think teachers can obtain from researching their own classroom practices?
- What constituted the "research" in this vignette and what constituted the "action"?

Purpose and benefits of action research

The day-to-day activities of teaching normally constitute a sufficiently demanding workload for most teachers, so an appropriate question is, why add research to a teacher's workload? Advocates of action research suggest that this concern reflects a misunderstanding of action research. Because action research is research based on teaching, it is best thought of as adding a research dimension to existing practice as a way to better understand and improve such practice. It also seeks to redefine the role of the teacher by giving teachers the means to set their own agendas for improvement and by shifting the responsibility for change or improvement from an outsider (a school board, a principal, a supervisor, a researcher) to teachers them-selves. As Sagor (1992, p. 5) comments, "By changing the role of teach-ers, we can profoundly change the teaching and learning process in our schools."

Teachers who have carried out action research often report significant changes to their understanding of teaching. For example, a teacher in Korea commented on his recent experiences with action research when he was teaching English to young learners.

Vignette

My first experience with action research was quite positive, dare I say enlightening? Two questions prompted my investigation. The topics were homework and student-teacher interaction. Both issues were problems at the time. Students often did not complete their homework. They claimed they hadn't enough time to complete their work, as they were busy with other classes and homework. The second issue dealt with teacher complaints that students were reluctant to interact during class. Teachers frequently com-plained that students were one-sided and lacked individual character and personality.

The solution? Write up a questionnaire investigating students' extracur-ricular activities, schedules, and free-time activities (and a number of related questions as well). The questionnaires were written in the students' L1 in order to accommodate less proficient students. The survey was given to 150 students at a private institute. They ranged in age from 8 years old through 17 years old. Additionally, 180 middle school students at a public school answered the survey. The results of the survey were enlightening. When shared with other staff members, the results were put to use, again with positive results that even dispelled cultural misperceptions.

The results of the survey went against current perceptions by students, parents, and teachers. Often parents claim that their children study con-stantly and have little time for extracurricular activities. Teachers, especially Western teachers, cling to the belief that their students attend private insti-tutes continuously from after school until late at night, often till midnight, which naturally led to the conclusion that students were tired, bored, and unmotivated.

However, students reported having sufficient time for excessive computer game playing, TV and video watching, sleeping, soccer, attending church, visiting downtown on weekends, chatting on the Internet with friends and strangers until 2 to 3 a.m., listening to music, and generally "killing time."

Only three respondents claimed to have a full schedule of private institutes or private lessons, thereby making my school's homework a difficult task to complete. It seems the others were "crying wolf." As a result, a homework policy was instituted. Within 6 months, homework completion rates were over 90 percent. The few who do not complete their homework prefer to stay after classes to do their homework regardless of penalties.

The other positive effect from this action research project was the introduction of cultural/age-based workshops in teacher-training meetings. The student interest reports were shown to teachers. Teachers then worked together to learn about topics of interest to students. This information was used by teachers in the class to promote student-teacher or student-student interaction, especially in times of silence caused by reluctant students or restrictive textbooks. Student motivation and participation increased. I no longer hear many teacher complaints that students lack character or are dull and apathetic. On the contrary, teachers now talk with enthusiasm about students' personal anecdotes in the teachers' room.

Why the positive results? Perhaps because the questionnaire, in L1, prompted the children and teenagers to feel important; perhaps because we, the school and teachers, were truly interested in them as real people and not as robotic students. That was my first experience with action research. The results may not be applicable to all young learner classes in every country, but in my context, the results are applicable. I have used the information to inform teachers to be more sensitive to young learner interests.

Action research has also given me a sense of professionalism and a desire to continue researching.

Jake Kimball

Reflection

- What sort of demands did Jake's research involve?
- What are the main benefits of the research (*a*) for the teacher and (*b*) for the learners?

Procedures used for conducting action research

Action research consists of a number of phases, which often recur in cycles:

- Planning
- Action

- Observation
- Reflection

The teacher (or a group of teachers):

1. Selects an issue or concern to examine in more detail (e.g., the teacher's use of questions).
2. Selects a suitable procedure for collecting information about the issue (e.g., recording classroom lessons).
3. Collects the information, analyzes it, and decides what changes might be necessary in his or her teaching.
4. Develops an action plan to help bring about the desired change in classroom behavior (e.g., a plan to reduce the frequency with which the teacher answers questions).
5. Observes the effects of the plan on teaching behavior (e.g., by recording a lesson and analyzing the teacher's questioning behavior) and reflects on its significance.
6. Initiates a second action cycle, if necessary. (Richards & Lockhart, 1994, pp. 12–13)

Burns (2002) expands this process to a cycle of eleven events that characterize action research projects she has conducted with teachers in Australia.

- *Exploring* (finding an issue to investigate)
- *Identifying* (analyzing the issue in more detail to understand it more fully)
- *Planning* (deciding what kind of data to collect about the issue and how to collect it)
- *Collecting data* (collecting data about the issue)
- *Analyzing/reflecting* (analyzing the data)
- *Hypothesizing/speculating* (arriving at an understanding based on the data)
- *Intervening* (changing classroom practice based on the hypothesis one arrived at)
- *Observing* (observing what happened as a result of the changes)
- *Reporting* (describing what one observed)
- *Writing* (writing up the results)
- *Presenting* (presenting the findings to other teachers)

Burns (2002, pp. 14–15) gives the following example of how these processes influenced the design of a collaborative action research project carried out by Burns and Cheryl Pfister (the teacher).

Vignette

Cheryl, a teacher from Hobart, Tasmania, wanted to develop a teaching program that would help her students to individualize their learning of English for specific purposes (ESP). She chose this focus because she had become increasingly aware of the frustration experienced by students who were unable to describe their vocational skills, experiences, and recreational interests because of a limited range of vocabulary. She realized that it did not seem to matter how competent a student was in general English, vocabulary in English for specific purposes (ESP) was consistently lacking.

With her post-beginner class she adopted a teaching approach which allowed her students to develop vocabulary on a topic of their choice. First, the students chose an area of specific vocabulary they wanted to develop through independent study. Next, Cheryl ensured that the students could get access to resources and made it clear that she was available to support them. She provided them with visual and reference materials, dictionaries, technical books, ESL/ESP textbooks, newspapers and journals, a variety of CD-ROMs, and computers with Internet access. Cheryl saw her role as helping the students to establish realistic, short-term, and achievable goals. She wanted the students to take responsibility for their own learning and establish self-monitoring strategies for assessing which words were appropriate and useful.

Cheryl then offered the students three classroom sessions with her. In these sessions, she drew attention to things such as vocabulary definitions and categories, verbs and phrases, and words and clauses in context. She encouraged the students to go outside the classroom for their projects, so they also made use of resources in the community. For example, one student spoke to a music student about how to read music, two students audited a tourism lecture at the local technical college, and another student spoke to a salesman in a car yard.

The ESP interests of the students were very varied and were based on their personal or career interests. They included Genetics, Biology, Travel and Tourism, Cards, Graphics in Computers, Guitars and Music, Soccer Clubs and Sponsorship, Journalism, Magnetism and Energy in Physics, Bangkok, the Structure and Operation of Import/Export Companies, and Enzymes in Humans.

Finally, Cheryl scheduled a fourth classroom session for students to present their work to others in the class. The presentations were an opportunity for them to display their new vocabulary. The students showed a great deal of inventiveness in the way they did their presentations: a song written and sung in English; an explanation of the computerized Galileo system of international travel and hotel reservations; a simulated bus tour of Bangkok; a car salesman giving a sales pitch; and a description of how to get a hot tip for a newspaper story.

To collect data, Cheryl monitored the students' responses to the course through discussions with individual students and her own observations. She also used a questionnaire to survey the students on where they got their new vocabulary. In order of importance and frequency these were books, the Internet, people, newspapers, brochures, visits, CD-ROMs, and other resources, such as video.

Cheryl argued that her new teaching approach means that the students become more confident in taking responsibility for ESP vocabulary development once they have been given a starting point and strategies. She concluded that ESP requires setting up opportunities, offering support, and, above all, trusting the students to use their time effectively.

Reflection

- What benefits do you think Cheryl obtained from her project?
- What are some other strategies she could have used to expand her students' vocabulary?

We will now examine in more detail the different steps normally involved in conducting action research.

Select an issue

Action research begins with a concern a teacher has about his or her classes or with an issue the teacher would like to explore and learn more about. The following are examples of issues that could be the focus of action research:

- Some of the students in my speaking class never seem to take part in speaking activities.
- No matter how many times I correct certain errors in my students' writing, they seem to continue making them.
- I'd like to change the way I do group work. It doesn't seem to be very effective in my classes.
- I'd like to know more about how I correct students' oral errors and whether my correction strategies are effective or not.

- I'd like to try out some collaborative learning techniques with my students.

In developing topics for action research, we emphasize the importance of choosing issues that can be fairly readily explored and that are likely to lead to practical follow-up. The focus of an action research project is an essential factor in determining its successful completion. Sagor (1992, p. 23) has remarked:

Teams who began their work with a clear idea of what they were studying and why they were studying it tended to find the motivation to complete their work. Conversely, the teams who lacked clarity on what they were about tended to lose interest in their collaborative work.

Once an issue or question has been identified, it needs to be made more specific in order for it to become part of an action research project. This involves turning it into a more specific question. Such a question will usually focus on some aspect of teaching, learner behavior, or the use of materials. For example, the issues just identified could be turned into the following more specific questions:

- Some of the students in my speaking class never seem to take part in speaking activities.
  More specific question:
  What kinds of speaking activities involve all of the class in speaking?
- No matter how many times I correct certain errors in my students' writing, they seem to continue making them.
  More specific question:
  What change in error correction strategies might improve the accuracy of students' writing?
- I'd like to change the way I do group work. It doesn't seem to be very effective in my classes.
  More specific question:
  What procedures for using group work will work well with my learners?
- I'd like to know more about how I correct students' oral errors and whether my correction strategies are effective or not.
  More specific question:
  What error correction strategies do I use in my oral classes and how effective are they?
- I'd like to try out some collaborative learning techniques with my students.
  More specific question:
  How effective are collaborative learning activities with my students?

A decision must also be made as to whether the issue chosen can be explored on one's own or whether it is best explored in collaboration with other teachers. Some proponents of action research argue that it is always best viewed as a collaborative activity, and indeed, the practical difficulties of carrying out action research are often best resolved through a team approach. Nevertheless, many teachers we have worked with have also reported successful experiences with individual action research projects.

Collect information about the issue

In order to further explore some aspect of teaching, it is first necessary to collect information on what the current characteristics of one's teaching are or what is happening in the classroom in relation to the issue in question. For example, in relation to the specific questions just identified, the following information could be collected:

1. *What kinds of speaking activities involve all of the class in speaking?* In order to investigate this question, it will be necessary to determine what speaking activities you currently use and the types of interaction and language use they generate. Lessons could be audiotaped or videotaped to provide this information.
2. *What change in error correction strategies might improve the accuracy of students' writing?* This question requires collecting information on the types of error correction strategies you currently use and their effects on learner performance. Alternative strategies can be tried and monitored for their effects.
3. *What procedures for using group work will work well with my learners?* Here it will be necessary to find out how you currently use group work and what problems group work currently poses. By systematically varying characteristics of group work, such as preparation activities, group size, and group membership, more effective group-work strategies can be determined.
4. *What error correction strategies do I use in my oral classes and how effective are they?* Again, this question requires collecting information on the types of error correction strategies you currently use through audiotaping or videotaping lessons, trying alternative strategies, and monitoring their effectiveness.
5. *How effective are collaborative learning activities with my students?* This could start with a description of the type of teaching you currently do and the type of classroom interaction that typically characterizes your lessons. Lessons could then be taught using

collaborative learning procedures and the two approaches to teaching compared.

Knowing what the intended outcome of the research is will often help the teacher decide on what issue to investigate. Is it for the teacher's own interest? Is it in order to resolve a problem that is common in the school? Is it a topic the teacher would like to present at a seminar or write about in a newsletter?

There are two points at which data will normally need to be collected: before carrying out the action research, and after the research strategy has been implemented. Data collected before the action research enables one to examine the issue or problem in depth in order to arrive at a way of addressing the problem. Data collected after the intervention will enable the teacher to decide if the action taken solved the problem.

There are many different ways of collecting data on classroom events. Burns (1999, p. 79) includes the following as examples of observational approaches to collecting classroom data:

- *Notes*. Descriptions and accounts of observed events, including nonverbal information, physical settings, group structures, interactions between participants
- *Diaries/journals*. Regular dated accounts of teaching/learning plans, activities, and events, including personal philosophies, feelings, reactions, reflections, explanations
- *Recordings*. Audio or video recordings providing objective records of classroom interactions
- *Transcripts*. Written representations of recordings, using conventions for identifying speakers and indicating pauses, hesitations, overlaps, and nonverbal information
- *Diagrams*. Maps or drawings of the classroom indicating physical layout and/or student-teacher interactions or locations

Other nonobservational methods of collecting information may also be needed, such as:

- *Interviews and discussions*. Face-to-face personal interactions that generate data about the research issue and allow specific issues to be discussed from other people's perspectives
- *Questionnaires and surveys*. Written sets of questions used to gain responses to non-face-to-face situations (usually focused on specific issues and may invite either factual or attitudinal responses)

- *Life/career histories.* Profiles of students' previous life and learning experiences told from the perspective of the individuals concerned and which may be compiled over a period of time
- *Documents.* Collections of various documents relevant to the research questions, which can include students' written work, student records and profiles, course overviews, lesson plans, and classroom materials

There are, of course, advantages and disadvantages to each form of data collection. Some procedures allow a large amount of information to be collected fairly quickly (e.g., a questionnaire), whereas others take more time but allow for more in-depth information to be collected (e.g., an interview). It is important that the information collected be reliable, that is, that the procedures used measure what they claim to measure and measure it accurately. One way to ensure this is by collecting information from several different sources about the issue that is being investigated. This is known as *triangulation*. Sagor (1992, p. 44) gives this example:

Say I wanted to investigate my use of cooperative learning structures in my classroom. I might choose to have a colleague observe my class, I might evaluate my own performance as captured on a videotape, and I might have another colleague interview my students. If all three windows on my cooperative learning lesson ended up showing the same picture, then that picture is a valid portrait of my teaching.

As a result of collecting information about the question that was being investigated, the teacher is now in a position to examine the information and try to make sense of it. This involves sifting through the data to find out what the most important themes are which emerge from it. For example, imagine that the following information was collected in response to the issues and questions discussed above:

1. *Current practices in regard to speaking activities*
   Findings: Discussion tasks in pairs were the primary means of encouraging discussion in class and group problem-solving tasks were less frequently observed (limited to 10 percent of the time).
2. *Error correction strategies used in correcting students' writing*
   Findings: Teacher corrected all grammar errors 100 percent of the time; use of underlining and symbols to indicate errors; students corrected errors by writing corrected words only; they did not rewrite the essay.
3. *Group-work procedures*
   Findings: Teacher modeled the task prior to group work and the students practiced what was expected. All group participants (groups of four) were assigned roles prior to discussion: group leader, group recorder, group timekeeper.

4. *Effectiveness of error correction strategies*
   Findings: The primary mode of error correction observed was when the teacher interrupted the learner and provided the correct language example. Some students self-corrected about 5 percent of the time.
5. *Classroom interaction patterns*
   Findings: Teacher-fronted and whole-class teaching observed 80 percent of the time; 20 percent of the time students were interacting with each other in pairs or in groups. Desks set up in rows.

Develop an action plan and observe its effects

On the basis of the information collected about the current situation, a plan can be developed for acting on this information to bring about changes in the classroom. Action research sets out with the explicit aim of improving teaching and learning. Because action research is often tentative and exploratory, it can go through two or more cycles (see Figure 12.1). This means that the cycle can take place in a spiral rather than in sequential steps.

As a result of identifying a problem and collecting information about it, the teacher is in a position to try to do something about it. This will normally involve making changes in the way the teacher teaches, in the materials he or she makes use of, or in the forms of assessment that are employed. Once a strategy for implementing the change has been developed, it then needs to be implemented in the classroom and the effects of the change observed. For example, the five example issues discussed in the preceding section could lead to changes in the way group work and error correction are carried out. This could be followed up by investigation of the effects of these changes on classroom participation patterns and error rate. Often, however, an initial change of teaching strategy, materials, or form of assessment, leads to a further cycle of changes and monitoring, as several successive strategies are tried out. The following vignette illustrates how a teacher adopted this process of action research to look at his questioning behavior in his classes.

Vignette
For a long time I was curious about the number and type of questions I asked in my English conversation classes. However, I never really had the time to

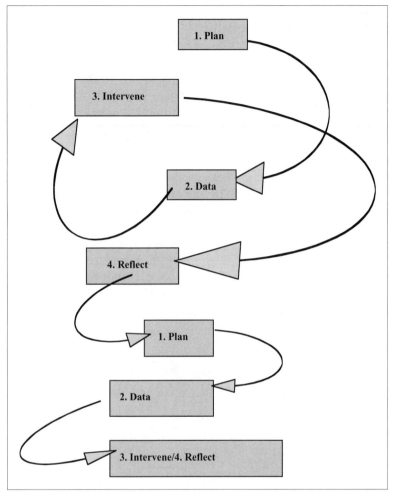

Figure 12.1: **Cycle of action research.** Plan, gather data, intervene, reflect, plan, gather data, intervene, reflect...

look into this issue. Anyway, one day I was determined to investigate this issue and I even asked my colleagues at the same school if they were curious or interested in joining me in looking at this issue. One colleague said she was interested and so I said I would read up a bit on the issue of teacher questioning behavior in ESL classes. I read a few articles in the library and was surprised to see that teachers generally ask "display"-type questions – we teachers already know the answer to the questions we ask – rather than asking more intellectually demanding questions ("referential questions" that we do not know the answer to before we ask). I invited my colleague to come observe my listening comprehension class one day. I was using CBS's *60 Minutes* TV show – 15-minute segments of news. I planned to show one 15-minute segment twice. I asked my colleague to write down every question I asked during this class. After the class, my colleague and I discussed the number and type of questions I had asked. To my great surprise, I learned that I had asked forty-five questions during the time the tape was not playing – in 15 minutes before and after the tape-playing. Furthermore, my colleague showed me that forty of these questions were of the "display" type. With this new information about my questioning behavior in the classroom, I decided that I wanted to change the number and type of questions I asked in my listening comprehension classes. I decided to write down a few (ten) referential-type questions that I would ask during the next class and I again invited my colleague to observe. After the class, my colleague noted that I did, in fact, ask the ten referential questions I had prepared and that these questions generated more discussion (sustained) in the class. I am more sensitive now about the number of questions I ask in class and the different types of questions that can generate different types of answers from my students.

Eric Harmsen

Reflection

- What were the benefits of transcribing the sections of the lesson the teacher was interested in?
- What other strategies could the teacher have used to change his questioning behaviors?

Share the findings with others

Part of the philosophy of action research is sharing the results of the research with other colleagues. This both leads to a better understanding of the findings and helps "build a community of practitioners aligned towards teacher research and a professional climate that is open to public scrutiny and constructive critique" (Burns, 1999, p. 183). The results of an action research project can be shared in a number of ways:

- an oral or written presentation to colleagues
- writing an article for a teacher's magazine

- communicating with an Internet forum or discussion group
- giving a workshop
- creating and displaying a poster about the action research
- preparing a video presentation about the action research

Implementing action research

In planning action research, it is useful to keep these questions in mind:

1. *Purpose*. Why am I starting this action research project? Is it to solve a problem that has occurred in my classroom? Or is it something else?
2. *Topic*. What issue am I going to investigate? What is going on in my classes that is causing me concern?
3. *Focus*. How can I narrow down the issue to investigate to make it manageable within a specific time frame? What is the precise question I am going to ask myself?
4. *Mode*. How am I going to conduct the research? What data-collecting methods will I need and why?
5. *Timing*. How much time will it take and how much time do I have?
6. *Resources*. What are the resources, both human and material, that I can call upon to help me complete the research? How can my institution help?
7. *Product*. What is the likely outcome of the research, as I intend it?
8. *Action*. What action will I expect to take as a result of conducting this research? How will I carry out this action?
9. *Reporting*. How will I share the finding of this research with other teachers? What forum will I use for this and why?

Summary

Action research can be a powerful way for language teachers to investigate their own practice. It is usually undertaken with the idea of improving a teacher's classroom practice. This type of research requires that the teacher investigate an issue that he or she has been puzzled by for a period of time by engaging in a process of planning, action, observation, and reflection. As a result of insight gained from undertaking an action research project, language teachers not only learn a lot about their own teaching but can also become more expert at investigating their own practice. Teachers can also share their results with other teachers by going to conferences or publishing their work in language teaching journals. In this way, other teachers may be encouraged to explore their own teaching by replicating these action research projects or by carrying out new action research studies on topics and issues they consider important or even unique to their particular contexts.

Examples of action research

1. The reflective cycle

Sabrina Almeida Ribeiro

SETTING

Most language teachers would agree that the communicative approach emphasizes fluency, and minor inaccuracies should be overlooked. This, however is only the first step of an approach that is truly communicative: Once students have reached a satisfactory level of fluency, what was once overlooked should be reconsidered so that communication can become even more effective. For this reason, not even the most "communicative" teachers should neglect accuracy, or forget to raise their students' awareness about their "growth edges" as language learners.

Having been a teacher for 10 years in Brazil, I frequently encounter the problem of the "intermediate plateau" in many of my learners. It seems that even though students visibly improve their rate of delivery, mistakes keep recurring in the same basic structures. Furthermore, most of the new vocabulary presented at their level becomes passive, and learners continue using words of Latin origin that resemble Portuguese. I decided to investigate this problem, and reflect upon how my teaching could motivate my learners to improve their language skills.

FOCUS

A lot has been written on the topic of striking a balance between fluency and accuracy in second language learning. It is not difficult to find books or articles full of enlightened ideas and practical procedures to be carried out in the classroom. I decided to follow the hints given in a number of

An earlier version of this paper first appeared in *New Routes Magazine* 16 (January 2002), pp. 26–29.

books at my disposal, and to monitor the performance of the students in an intermediate group at CEL-LEP, a language school in São Paulo.

When I started teaching this group, my expectations about their English were quite high, as they were in the last stage of the intermediate course. What I found out, however, was that despite their openness and enthusiasm for learning, they were careless when speaking and unwilling to try new discussion topics that contained unlearned lexis. Once on task, most were blithely inaccurate in their communicative strategies, once they were able to figure out the aim and focus of the tasks in class. I did not want to tell them to feel ashamed about their level of English proficiency, but I wanted to find a way to encourage accuracy as well as fluency.

INVESTIGATION

The tools aiding my research were audio recordings of my classes and feedback questionnaires from students. The first issue to be investigated was my teaching. For that, the plan was to make an audio recording of one of my lessons. The aim was to look at my attitude toward error correction, teacher and student talking time, pace, and rapport, and to analyze the quality of the learners' language production, as well as their most frequent mistakes. After all the data was collected, the next step would be to establish action plans for any area that I felt needed improvement.

Listening to the recording, I found out that my error correction was not as effective as I hoped it to be. The reason for that was that many times students were so engaged in what they wanted to say that they either did not pay attention, or were unaware of my corrections. It became clear that I needed to prepare my class to be more open and receptive to correction, because no matter how much I could improve my methods for offering instruction to learners, if they were not open to it, intake would be minimal.

During the following class, I took the recorder again. This time, I told them the focus would be on their English. A new recording was made for each communicative activity in class. I listened to the recordings at home, and made a list of some of the mistakes they had made. In the beginning of the following class, I showed them the list, and asked them to correct it in pairs. After we had gone over all the utterances, I asked them to spot the mistakes on the list they thought they had made. Then I asked them to choose one error they did not want to make again in that week, circle it and return the list to me (see Figure 12.2).

That week, I paid a lot of attention to what the learners said. The following week, I gave each of them the sheets back, with a little feedback note that

LEARNING DIARY

NAME:_____

In pairs, correct these mistakes. Then spot the ones you have made, and choose ONE mistake you don't want to make again.

Mistakes   Correct form

1. There is a lot of bizarre excuses.
2. I've got to take my grandmother to bingo.
3. When I don't want do something I gave the
   person a lot of excuses, but not strange excuses.
4. You don't need be on a diet.
5. I stopped to eat a lot.
6. I changed my mind to loose weight.
7. I have a strong hurt in my back.
8. I arrived to the doctor crying.
9. I never know say this word.
10. We bring to class with another ideas.
11. If I had started more serious in the past, study
    English, I would be in a better position.
12. A head Ferrari.
13. I know her since seven grade. Six years.
14. She has eyes of Japanese.

Figure 12.2

either offered praise or my observations of how many times the wrong form had come up.

This new procedure served its purpose, not only of the correction itself, but also of showing the students some strategies that they could use independent of the teacher.

RESPONSE

Geared to reach my goal of learner training, I prepared a form (Figure 12.3) where learners could keep weekly records of their mistakes and the correct forms. I encouraged them to choose only one form for each lesson. In that way, learning would be focused, personal, and meaningful.

Sometime later, I made the recordings again. This time, I asked the students to listen to the recordings and prepare a list of mistakes the class had made. They would then select the errors on which they wanted to focus. We recorded a fluency activity that was part of the planned lesson and listened to it during the last 15 minutes of class. Students had to raise their hands every time they thought they had heard a mistake, and then discuss

---

LEARNER DIARY

Date   What I said (or wrote)   Best form

Figure 12.3

the most suitable correction. At the start, they were embarrassed to point out other students' errors, but by the end of the activity, students were pleased, as there was no atmosphere of criticism or judgment.

I used the audio recording once more, but later on during the course so that it did not become repetitive, and with a slightly different purpose. Students were recorded giving simple directions to each other, and then they participated in a vocabulary expansion activity. At the end of the activity, they were recorded giving directions again. Without focusing on correction, their final task was to listen for changes and for richer vocabulary.

At the end of this cycle of action research, I developed a feedback questionnaire to discover the students' impressions of the process (see Appendix). I was very happy to find out that they could notice progress in their learning.

REFLECTIONS

Hubbard, P., Jones, H., Thornton, B., and Wheeler, R. (1985, p. 37) state that "every language teacher should begin by considering what the aims of his pupils are, both in the short and the long run, and judge the success by whether these are achieved." The main advantage of what was accomplished in this reflective cycle was to equip students with the tools necessary for observing their performance. As I reflect personally upon this action re-search project, I believe that a teacher's focused awareness of what is taking place in the classroom is the greatest contributing factor to raising students' awareness. The more the teacher is driven to reflect upon and deal with what is happening in the classroom, the greater the chance of students noticing issues about their own learning.

Some might claim that teachers should not expose students to the wrong forms they have produced, that this could reinforce the storage and retrieval of that form. However, I strongly believe that learners should be able to recognize, notice, and compare both correct and marked forms of the target language. Often as learners, understanding why something is wrong can aid us in making the right language decisions. This reflection helped me understand that, as language teachers, we should make more room in our instruction for the teaching of learning strategies. Doing so will empower students to learn independently from the teacher, and to make the most of their classroom experience.

2. Discovering the classroom community

David Mayo

SETTING

I teach at a private college in Japan; my students are young women studying English for its general value in international communication. I have long admired the hard-won accomplishments of people striving to learn the language without, in most cases, experiencing life in the environment where it is widely used. My students' needs are in many ways similar to learners in other Asian EFL settings, where an enduring cultural dynamic influences the quality of interaction in language classrooms.

In Japan, as in other rice-based Asian societies, close cooperation among neighbors was indispensable. Heavy dependence on others, while mutually beneficial, tended to inhibit people from pursing their personal goals for fear of the disapproval or ridicule of their community. With industrialization, it soon became necessary for many Japanese to adapt to an educational system in which, from secondary school onward, they must function as individuals competing for coveted careers. They lost the benefits of neighborly cooperation, yet remained haunted by the vulnerability to "people's eyes": now, the eyes of rivals rather than protectors.

FOCUS

The implicit view of students as solitary runners in a race pervades even women's colleges, where competitive pressure is relatively light and social relations thrive. Like other teachers, I have tried to relieve the academic isolation of students in my own classes by reviving the principle of cooperation.

I had often adopted two forms of student cooperation that are common in EFL classes: small groups (typically, four students) and pairs. I had found each form good in its way, at least for tasks that were product-oriented. I felt the need to rethink cooperation while planning a new course that valued more student initiative in the process of learning. Learners in the new course were organized into groups of four for discussion, writing, and oral reporting.

INVESTIGATION

To evaluate the small-group arrangement as a basis for student-centered learning, I decided to keep a classroom diary: a research instrument that necessitates simultaneously supervising class activities and recording detailed observations of them for later analysis (Nunan, 1989, pp. 55–60). Although difficult, I could do this while observing students as they worked in groups.

Keeping the diary began before the first class, with a long entry on the preparation of the course. Here, I attempted to establish certain objectives for the research project that roughly corresponded to those of the course. This "early reflection" served to maximize the usefulness of the classroom observations, while giving me a chance to avoid errors in the course design. Because the course rewarded highly motivated students with satisfying and productive opportunities to use English, I wanted to be alert to the factors affecting the active participation of individual students. I devised the following framework for my classroom diary entries:

1. *Aims*

    Each day's record begins with a statement of aims for that day.

2. *Attendance*

    As the success of group work may depend on regular participation, each record will note the absence of group members.

3. *Events*

    The main section of each record will report the events of the day's class, consistently noting the attainment of specific aims and apparent student satisfaction.

It was important to report classroom events as they unfolded, thereby capturing my own immediate impressions and responses. As a secondary measure to ensure accuracy and to compensate for unavoidable lapses in real-time reporting, all classes were recorded on audiotape cassettes. Repeated listening to portions of these recordings also enriched my analysis of the diary.

The value of data obtained from this kind of research is something akin to the psychoanalytic process of bringing buried knowledge to light. The observations set down in the Events section of my diary soon began to show a progressively incisive narrative pattern. Some excerpts:

Day 2: ... students finish reading but do not start talking. I realize that I have made a mistake in failing to give them a discussion mechanism. I suggest that they should first choose their representative. Then she will solicit the impressions of the others and jot them down as a basis for the report.

Day 3: They tend to write their remarks for the representative to consolidate, instead of having a discussion. The representative of Group 2 is a very capable student, but when I prompt her to get something started, she just gives me a knowing look.

Day 12: Group 2 still has trouble getting under way, although the members seem well enough acquainted now. They tend to sit and stare at the papers till I sit down and work with them. ... I think I know the cause of the awkwardness here. Unlike the other groups, each of which includes one student who can serve as "big sister" to the rest, this one includes three such students. They recognize each other's ability, respect it, and endlessly defer to it.

This conscious accumulation and refinement of observations revealed students' needs that might have escaped my notice if I had been present only as a teacher and not as a teacher-researcher. In some groups, the students apparently needed freedom from the necessity of performing before the "eyes" of certain peers, because they either lacked self-confidence or felt that displaying their superior ability would be alienating. In Group 2, three proficient students simply needed to seek cooperation unselfconsciously. They ultimately became good friends who enjoyed combining their strengths. It seemed that I had obstructed that development by throwing them together with the implicit command to "cooperate."

RESPONSE

This new insight led me to look for an alternative to small groups as a way of promoting cooperation in the learning process. With the ultimate aim of realizing differentiated classes in which "both what is learned and the learning environment are shaped to the learner" (Tomlinson, 1999, p. 2), I designed a flexible collaborative learning arrangement that balances mutual support with individual initiative more dynamically than the small-group model.

There are no established groups. Instead, students working on individual learning tasks are free to move about the room and consult one another as neighbors or coworkers do, to form ad hoc groups, or to work alone. Although encouraged to seek each other's help in the learning process, they are responsible for demonstrating effective engagement in their own tasks. I have subsequently adopted a modified form of this arrangement in other classes. By allowing mutual assistance to take place spontaneously, free collaboration opens the way for wholehearted support between classmates who might not be grouped together otherwise.

REFLECTION

Many writers have advocated the organization of students in small groups as an alternative to teacher-fronted classes. Since the mid-1990s, the status of group work in communicative language teaching methodology has been so secure that a list of its advantages might be juxtaposed with "excuses for avoiding group work," every one of which was disallowed (Brown, 1994, pp. 173–178). Nevertheless, the insight gained from this action research project has prompted me to move beyond classroom procedures based on work groups. As I reflect on my findings, I believe there are two weaknesses in the group work principle.

First, it has an authoritarian aspect that may go unnoticed by teachers intent on promoting learner autonomy. If one accepts that the teacher decides the form and composition of groups, then one should also accept that some students would be obliged to cooperate unwillingly. The problem is unsolved by letting the students form their own groups, because it remains understood that all must do so.

Second, adding a grouping ritual to more traditional classroom rituals achieves only a minor relaxation of form. The prearranged group of four, with its facing desks and its imposed relationships, is hardly less rigid a concept than the teacher-fronted class. These reasons lead me to believe that the small-group model was a fundamentally flawed expression of the teacher's will in promoting learner autonomy.

This action research helped me to become more attentive to the principle of collaboration, which stresses mutuality among responsible individuals rather than mere labor-sharing (Roschelle & Teasley, 1995). I was able to bring this principle to bear on the larger task of meeting the different needs of individual students in my classes.

Like throwing new light on an old scene, this action research project illuminated the possibility of enabling students to collaborate in a more natural way. As classroom neighbors sharing insights, and new ideas, my learners were able to enjoy the fruits of language learning in a way that complemented their cultural values.

References and further reading

Brown, H. (1994). *Teaching by principles: An interactive approach to language pedagogy.* Englewood Cliffs, NJ: Prentice Hall Regents.

Burns, A. (1999). *Collaborative action research for english language teachers.* Cambridge: Cambridge University Press.

Burns, A. (2002). Teachers' voices: Exploring action research in Australia. *New Routes Magazine* (São Paulo) (July 2002) 18, pp. 12–15.

Hubbard, P., Jones, H., Thornton, B., & Wheeler, R. (1983). *A training course for TEFL.* Oxford: Oxford University Press.

Mayo, D. (2003). Discovering the classroom community. In G. Hadley (Ed.), *Asian voices: Action research in action* (pp. 16–20). Portfolio series, v. Singapore: SEAMEO Regional Language Centre.

Nunan, D. (1989). *Understanding language classrooms.* Hemel Hempstead: Prentice Hall.

Patterson, L., Minnick Santa, C., Short, K., & Smith, K. (Eds.). (1993). *Teachers are researchers: Reflection and action.* Newark, DE: International Reading Association.

Pfister, C. (2001). Developing ESP vocabulary in the ESL classroom. In A. Burns & H. de Silva (Eds.), *Teachers voices 7: Teaching vocabulary* (pp. 39–45). Sydney: National Centre for English Language Teaching and Research.

Ribeiro, S. A. (2002). The reflective cycle. *New Routes Magazine* 16 (January), pp. 26–29.

Richards, J. C., & Lockhart, C. (1994). *Reflective teaching in second language classrooms.* New York: Cambridge University Press.

Roschelle, J., & Teasley, S. (1995). The construction of shared knowledge in collaborative problem solving. *In S. O'Malley (Ed.) Computer supported collaborative learning* (pp. 69–97). Berlin: Springer-Verlag.

Sagor, R. (1992). *How to conduct collaborative action research.* Alexandria, VA: Association for Supervision and Curriculum Development.

Tomlinson, C. (1999). *The differentiated classroom: Responding to the needs of all learners.* Alexandria, VA: Association for Supervision and Curriculum Development.

Wallace, M. J. (1998). *Action research for language teachers.* Cambridge: Cambridge University Press.

Appendix

Feedback Questionnaire

STUDENT FEEDBACK

Name: _____

1. Think of something you can do now that you couldn't do in the beginning of the course. Then write or draw it.
2. How much has your English improved in each of these areas? Mark the appropriate box.

	A lot of improvement	Some improvement	Little improvement
Speaking			
Listening			
Reading			
Writing			
Grammar			
Vocabulary			

3. Which area do you think you need to focus more on?

_____

_____

4. What can you do to improve your English in these areas?

Speaking			
Listening			
Reading			
Writing			
Grammar			
Vocabulary			

5. Mark the appropriate box.

Have you been:	Yes	Sometimes	No
coming to classes regularly?			
participating orally?			
going to the lab regularly?			
doing your written work?			
doing anything extra?			

6. What class activities did you like best?

_____

_____

7. What suggestions would you like to make?

_____

_____

TEACHER FEEDBACK

_____

_____

Index

An italic number refers to information inside tables, charts, or figures.